*How to Create Meaningful
and Lasting Change in Your Life*

V CTOR
NOT
VICTIM

*How to Create Meaningful
and Lasting Change in Your Life*

VICTOR
NOT
VICTIM

Dr. Aleksander Šinigoj

SUMMIT PRESS

Printed in the United States of America
First Printing, 2025
ISBN: 979-8-9852063-4-0
Library of Congress number: 2025902162

Summit Press Publishers
P.O. Box 1356
Intervale, New Hampshire 03845

For information about special discounts available for bulk purchase, workshops, retreats, and webinars associated with this book or offered by Aleksander Šinigoj, please contact him at www.aleksandersinigoj.com.

To my wife, Petra, and our children Matic, Ema, Žiga, and Ana.
May you always believe in yourself.

TABLE OF CONTENTS

———

INTRODUCTION

———

Life isn't about finding yourself; life is about creating yourself.
–George Bernard Shaw

We humans fall into the habit of playing victim from time to time. I can't think of a single more unproductive way of thinking and behaving. When you experience lack in your life, the likely culprit lurks within victimhood.

So, today is the day you stop playing the role of victim.

Today is the start of your new life, the one in which you consistently produce the results you previously thought impossible. This is the moment you begin to turn self-doubt and fear into power—the power to do what's needed to achieve success.

Today you take the first steps toward moving your life to the next level, changing how you respond to life's challenges, harnessing the power of self-control, mastering the art of goal setting, and winning your inner battles.

I'm thrilled you're joining me on this journey.

There is absolutely no reason you can't have all that you aspire to, regardless of your current circumstances. Your big breakthrough is right around the corner.

By breakthrough, I'm talking a significant advancement or achievement in a particular area of your life. It's a moment of clarity, insight, or innovation that leads to a notable shift in understanding, perspective, or progress. It can occur in various aspects of life, from personal development to creative endeavors. And it can play a crucial role in facilitating progress by helping you zero in on the underlying cause of challenges or barriers that are preventing you from following through on your goals or desired changes.

When you experience a breakthrough, it ignites motivation and inspiration, which can energize you to act and persist, even in the face of adversity.

In short, a breakthrough serves as a catalyst for change by providing clarity, motivation, problem-solving abilities, confidence, and momentum. Learn to embrace and leverage those breakthrough moments; chances are good you already know what you should be doing to create meaningful and lasting change in your life—so, empower yourself to overcome your obstacles and get it done . . .

Trapped in a Rut

There's nothing worse than knowing what you should do but not doing it. My whole life, I've dreamed of consistently taking right actions, of not succumbing to procrastination or giving up before my goals were achieved. I'm not alone in my desire for straight-line, resistance-free improvement. After all, most people who set New Year's Resolutions don't stick to them. They revert to old habits before the month of January is over.

The problem has little to do with a lack of desire.

Everywhere I turn, I see people with the very life sucked out of them by daily drudgery. They dislike their job, yet they get up early in the morning and head to work anyway. They perform tasks they don't particularly enjoy and for which they receive little compensation. They dream of more money, more respect, but do little about it. After work, they return home where they're trapped in an unhappy relationship. Instead of dealing with it, they flip on the TV or waste time on social media. They know that the food they eat is unhealthy and doesn't provide the energy their body needs. They know better. And they want more for themselves, yet they're caught in a vicious cycle from which they can't seem to break free . . . as long as they are playing the victim.

In many ways, I was trapped in the same rut. At first, I thought I had to put up with the status quo because I lacked money. Before long, there was a mile-long list of excuses for why I couldn't improve my situation and follow a plan of action. It's an easy out when you don't see any progress in your life: hunt for excuses, feel sorry for yourself, whine and complain, and spin like a hamster on a wheel.

It brings to mind the adage, "Insanity is doing the same thing over and over and expecting different results."

But then I began to wonder: *what causes some people to be successful while others aren't; why are some joyful and full of life while others suffer and spend their lives on autopilot; how do those born into disadvantaged circumstances—who endured constant physical or emotional abuse as children—change their lives to find happiness, success, and joy, while those born with everything they need to thrive in life—the greatest education, wealth, and living conditions—fail in their careers, relationships, finances, and other areas.*

What is the secret to creating the life you most want?

Looking around, I knew it wasn't about circumstances. So, I set out to uncover the secret because I realized, if I could harness its power, I could have what I truly wanted. I could overcome difficult situations and achieve my goals. I could interrupt the cycle and experience a real breakthrough. I could take the most effective and efficient actions to reach my goals quicker, with less resistance.

It happened for me; it can happen for you too.

Maybe you feel stuck in a vicious cycle, longing for a very different life than the one you currently live.

Maybe you find no fulfillment in your career.

Maybe you are or were a victim of physical or verbal abuse and are now coping with negative energy, unpleasant emotions, or blockages that seem to cloud everything in your life, including your relationships.

Maybe your finances are keeping you down; you've never seemed to master the ability to earn more or manage your spending.

Maybe you find it challenging to maintain a healthy lifestyle, to eat healthy foods (in moderation), and workout.

Maybe it's . . .

Whatever the challenge, whatever rut you find yourself in, a breakthrough will help you escape procrastination, a sense of frustration, and bad habits—so you can move towards your goal and desired results.

The Fear is Real

Humans are creatures of habit. As such, we all have limiting beliefs that hold us back from creating the life we want to lead. It stems from a fear of the unknown, a fear of what could be. This is where the adage, "Better the devil you know than the devil you don't," comes from. That's why we often prefer the familiarity of our current (less than ideal) circumstances over the uncertainty of change.

So yes, moving outside of your comfort zone can be unsettling—and for many good reasons.

At the very least, stepping into unfamiliar territory is intimidating; there is little you truly know ahead of time and so much you simply cannot know until you are in the midst of it.

Your past plays a part as well. Negative experiences can leave lasting impressions. They can make you hesitant to take risks or make big changes for fear of repeating past mistakes or facing similar challenges again.

Then, there's the future. If you make a big change, you risk losing future stability and security, as well as relationships. You may need to invest money, or you may face financial instability during the transition; you may need to deviate from social norms or expectations, which may lead to resistance or disapproval from others. So, even if the change could lead to positive outcomes in the long run, the fear of such loss can hold you back.

Overall, the fear of making a big change in life is multifaceted and deeply rooted in psychological, social, and practical factors. Overcoming these fears requires a combination of courage, resilience, support, and strategic planning.

And that's precisely what this book will provide.

Reconnect with Your Dream

Between excuses and fears, it can be easy to forget what we've always wanted.

Over the last two decades or so, I've given talks on goal achievement and personal development on four continents and in numerous countries across the globe. I've helped thousands of people reconnect with their dreams and turn them into reality, one goal at a time.

Participants in my events have quit smoking, found a partner, improved their relationships, had a long-awaited baby, lost weight or reached their ideal weight, found a job, established a successful business, reintroduced passion and love into their romantic relationship, doubled or tripled their profits, and stopped being afraid of flying or public speaking. I've helped many entrepreneurs, as well as those who want to establish their own business, get the traction they need, even in the most challenging times.

Sometimes these breakthroughs are large and visible right away. Shortly after attending one of my workshops, one participant doubled his company's turnover and, in a few years, began making over ten million dollars. Other times breakthroughs appear to be small and almost insignificant. One participant overcame abuserelated thoughts, another, limiting beliefs that kept her trapped in a no-win job. Each tiny win, each seemingly insignificant step toward their objective, became part of the larger mosaic of their success.

Yet when I talk to individuals about their desire for a breakthrough, they frequently claim that it's hard for them to even imagine having the outcome that they desire. They are unable to picture themselves on stage, giving a talk or presentation, writing a book. They can't see themselves as entrepreneurs. They can't picture themselves in a happy, fulfilling relationship, making their health and wellness a priority, having a job that's both satisfying and lucrative, doing what makes them happy. Some can't even imagine accomplishing the smallest of goals, of making the tiniest of transformations.

When people say they can't imagine changing, they are basically saying that they can't produce an image in their mind. It's an effortless activity that requires mere seconds. Think of a pink elephant. For a moment, your mind pictured a pink elephant, right? The same can be true for the desired change, result, or goal you want to achieve.

Others can see themselves starting—they can picture themselves meeting the right partner, getting a fulfilling job, or achieving their ideal weight—yet they can also see themselves failing at some point along the way. And because they envision an unhappy outcome, they never begin. It comes down to being able to say a few simple words: "I can do it! I will do this!" If you can't imagine saying these words, how will you actually realize them?

There is a way around roadblocks. All can change with a single thought.

So, what's your dream; what can you do . . . what will you do?

One Thought, One Action

Self-awareness is not for the faint of heart because it requires action. Yet it is often one single thought, one minor adjustment which serves as the catalyst to a breakthrough.

Once upon a time, my life was in shambles. Constantly playing the victim, I could not imagine succeeding in anything I set out to do. I felt powerless to change my circumstances; I believed external forces were responsible for my struggles and hardships and that I was at their mercy. I saw myself as the target of unfair treatment, discrimination, and injustice. I dwelt on past grievances and felt a sense of entitlement to sympathy or special treatment from others. At the same time, I saw myself as inherently flawed, unworthy, and inadequate. I struggled with low self-esteem, self-doubt, and feelings of hopelessness.

As a result of my poor mental state, self-concept, and terrible financial decision-making (both personally and professionally), I was deeply in debt. Unable to care for my family and loved ones, my identity as a man, father, husband, son—as someone who should be able to care for others—crumbled.

I wasn't sure what I was doing wrong. I worked hard, often to the point of exhaustion. Feeling constant pressure and fear of failure made me ill-tempered. Nothing in my life was changing; I was stuck in a vicious cycle as if banging my head against a wall. My thoughts were mostly negative.

Then one Christmas, I went to see my grandmother, empty-handed. Instead of handing me a gift, she gave me an envelope filled with money and told me to spend it on whatever I wanted or needed. When I looked at her old hands, worn from years of physical labor, and saw the pity in her eyes, I burst into tears. I couldn't stop crying. I should have been the one taking care of her and bringing her a present; instead, she was sacrificing for me.

Months later, I landed in the hospital because my heart seized on me. That's when I hit rock bottom. Alone in that hospital bed, I said to myself, "That's it. I'm done."

That's when I finally paused and listened to the call, which I had heard, whether consciously or unconsciously, many times in the past. I decided right then and there that I'd never again allow myself to be a victim or get into a similar situation. I knew that I could make it in business and take care of the people I love. I could rebuild my health to become stronger than ever so I wouldn't leave them in the lurch. This was and is my greatest "why," and it strengthened my will to breakthrough.

Of course, after that hospital stay, the real work began. For a period of time, I didn't have the slightest idea how or where to begin changing my life. Everything, it seemed, needed to be altered, which was too overwhelming. I wound up selecting health as the first area to focus on. I started eating healthier and incorporated exercise into my everyday routine.

As my health improved and the mental fog lifted, I began to pursue the field of personal development and fed my mind with thoughts that helped me focus on solutions and objectives. What started as a trip to the library became something of an addiction. Wanting to absorb all the wisdom available to help me move forward in life, I read, listened to audio books, studied; I sought out teachers, mentors, and coaches, and attended a number of workshops and seminars (even if I had to borrow money to do so). Sometimes I simply picked up a random book and opened it at a random page, and there was the message I needed to hear.

It has been a long road from where I started to where I am now, following my purpose with heart and energy. I'm publishing books (many of them in my first language), lecturing, and helping people all over the world. I help well-known, highly successful entrepreneurs overcome their unique version of limiting beliefs; and with numerous online and live events, I help participants attain their own breakthroughs. When I follow their successes and see how they're changing their lives and the lives of others for the better, I'm deeply grateful. Best of all, my work allows me to accomplish what I most wanted: to provide a living for my family and my team. And I do it all from a tiny, beautiful country on the sunny side of the Alps, Slovenia, tucked away in the very heart of Europe.

But I had to start.

So, let me tell you straight: nothing will change if *you* don't change something. There will be no progress if *you* don't act. Is now the right time to achieve a breakthrough in your area of concern; are you willing to move towards the results, goals, and everything that you wish to accomplish? The fact that you picked up this book is a good sign, but ultimately, it's a decision you need to make for yourself.

Prepare for the Journey

My goal is to inspire you to dream bigger: to first win that inner game, the precursor to winning the outer game, then to take the necessary actions to accomplish your dreams.

In full disclosure, what I'm about to share with you is not an overnight solution; it is a lifelong, satisfying journey. It's an interesting way of life.

I've learned and continue to learn from the greatest and most successful individuals from all around the world. I do so to better help those who seek my assistance. I plan to never stop learning; to continually improve so I can provide the most accurate, current, relevant, and practical knowledge to help my workshop attendees accomplish results in their lives. Their breakthroughs are a continual reminder that I'm on the right track, that I've latched onto my true purpose, which, given where I once was, feels miraculous.

Now I set big goals. And I achieve them. This is my passion for a couple of reasons. One, it's fun to evolve; two (and more importantly), I can't think of anything I want more than to help those who are suffering the way I once did. Helping others helps me live my best life.

At the risk of overstating what happened to me in that hospital, while I lay there fearing for my life, God (or if you want, the Universe) asked me to step into this role. With the monitors beeping all around me, I found myself inexplicably recalling the words of St. Francis of Assisi, "Lord, make me an instrument of your peace. Where there is hatred, let me sow love; where there is injury, pardon; where there is doubt, faith; where there is despair, hope; where there is darkness, light; and where there is sadness, joy."

In other words, my journey has taken on a life of its own. It has brought me places for which I had zero imagination.

I may not be smarter than you, but I have the thought process, and I've developed the tools to optimize outcomes. I've spent time analyzing exactly what needs to be done. I've created plans, acted on those plans, and achieved success. I've taught thousands of people how to do the same in a practical and clear way, within a specific time frame.

Now it's your turn.

By following this roadmap, you too will be able to:

- Unlock the power of your mind to achieve any kind of success.
- Conquer your hidden fear and take life to the next level.
- Master the art of goal setting.
- Win your inner battles.
- Rid yourself of old memories, thoughts, and beliefs that are holding you back and create a much more powerful story of who you are and what you are capable of accomplishing.
- Achieve insanely demanding goals.
- Unleash the potential within you.

In this book, you'll find the exact steps, tools, and inspiration to become a gold-medal champion, or whatever is your next level of success. It doesn't matter where you are: the starting line or the home stretch, unable to visualize what you're after or with goals as clear as day, feeling trapped in a maze with no way out or simply wanting to accomplish breakthroughs at a faster pace. This book (along with additional training videos and resources at http://aleksandersinigoj.com/victor) is for you.

Maybe you know exactly what must be done, and how, yet you procrastinate. You wait for a moment that's "just right" or perfect. Since that moment never arrives, you don't do what you know you should; since you don't change your behavior, you don't receive the outcomes you seek.

Well, I intend to help you fix that.

The only thing stopping you is your past and your current beliefs about what's possible. Remember, only trees with deep, strong roots can withstand a storm. Use this book as a guide to build a solid foundation for your own inner support. Believe in yourself and your mission—and you can't be stopped, no matter the obstacles life throws at you.

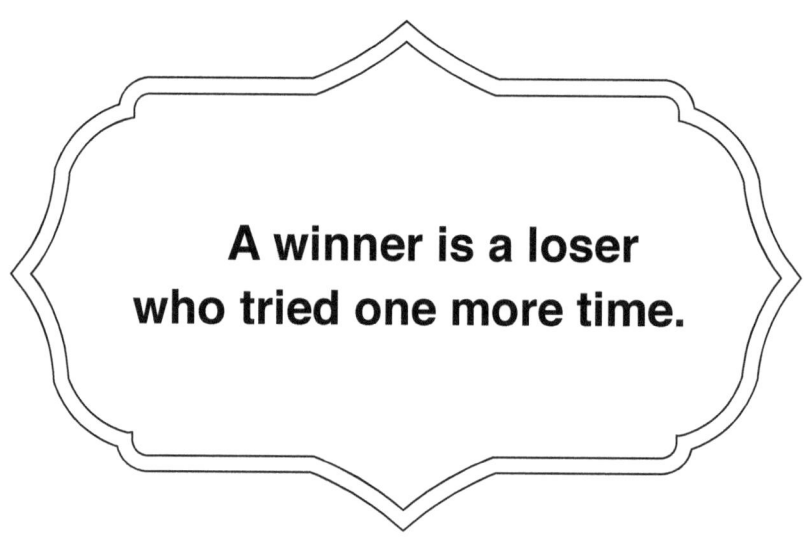

A winner is a loser
who tried one more time.

1

SETTING YOURSELF UP FOR YOUR BIG BREAKTHROUGH

A journey of a thousand miles must begin with a single step.

–Lao Tzu

A blond, short-haired woman showed up at one of my three-day workshops. So eager to discuss what had brought her there, when called upon, she failed to give her name. Instead, she launched right into a story about being without a job and needing to find a new one, which was proving to be quite challenging. According to her, the other employees in the company she worked for, her former employer, the coworkers in her department, the system, you name it, were all the problem, not her. The way she made it sound, they were somehow conspiring to keep her from landing on her feet. Without pause, she complained and complained and complained.

She could not see that she was completely unemployable. She operated in a bubble of beliefs that just didn't serve her or her cause. She would never find a job, given her penchant for blame. The moment she opened her mouth in an interview, out would pop a litany of things she found wrong. Her victim mentality shone bright and clear. She was going to be a tough nut to crack.

When it comes to my workshop participants, some are trapped in a vicious cycle; some don't respect themselves and allow others to mistreat them; some blindly chase after their goals, only to give up too soon; some procrastinate; and many, like that blond woman, are playing the victim. While these challenges may appear straightforward to an observer, they are often a blind spot for those struggling with them.

And therein lies the solution.

Before a breakthrough can take place, you must possess some sort of self-belief. If you've tried multiple times to accomplish your goals, to do what you know you should do, and have failed, I'm guessing faith in yourself is in short supply. But know this: the outcome you want could be as close as one thought away. You must first wrap your head around the fact that you can make a change; don't give up on yourself. Hear me out. A winner is simply a loser who tried one more time.

So, to set the stage for what's to come, let's take a moment to awaken a ray of hope, faith, and strength within yourself. Switch up the questions you're asking. Instead of, *why is this happening to me*; ask, *how can I put myself in a better frame of mind; or what qualities and behaviors do I need to improve? How can I rise from here with a smile?*

A little self-awareness can go a long way in preparing you for your big transformation.

The Antidote to Fear

Fear and doubt hold us back from creating the life that we want to lead, plain and simple. Probably the biggest fear, the granddaddy of them all, is that you may not believe that you're worthy of change and that success is possible for you. You have failed, miserably, probably more times than you can count. But there is an antidote to the fear of trying again: faith. Have faith in yourself.

Fear says, "What if . . ."

Faith says, "Even if . . ."

Fear looks for reasons to stop; faith looks for ways to continue. Gaining faith in yourself after experiencing setbacks or failures can be challenging, but it's entirely possible. Yet, you must maintain the faith that change is possible. Keep believing that you can do it. Keep believing that there's still a lot of potential within you. Because it's true. Perhaps you gave up at a certain time in your life because you believed you wouldn't make it, that you weren't deserving of success or meant to have a better life. By maintaining your faith and hope, you ensure that the light in your life continues to shine. Never give up on yourself or your life; never give up on mankind or your bright and promising future.

Some time ago, an elderly lady came to see me. Her husband, with whom she has twenty-one grandchildren, brought her because she hadn't been able to sleep for years due to restless legs syndrome. Her legs would shake so violently when she tried to relax that sleep eluded her, even with sleeping pills. The night before she visited me (and later for a special meditation recording I made for her), she slept through the night for the first time in years.

When I asked her what had happened, she said she had hope and faith that her problem would finally be resolved. I hadn't done anything yet, but the hope and faith were so strong that the change began even before we met. Have faith, have hope, that you already have within you all the resources you need to make the desired change in your life. Even if you don't have enough knowledge or understanding of everything that needs to be done, with persistence, desire, hard work, and learning, you can achieve your goals. Have faith.

Now, when I encourage you to have faith, to believe in yourself, which I will consistently repeat, you may assume I think it's easy to do. I can tell you from experience, it is not.

If you had asked me years ago, as I lay in that hospital bed, to help you obtain results and attain your goals, I would have laughed in your face (albeit politely). I couldn't have told you the first place to start. Regarding reprograming the mind, for which I'm primarily known, and transforming oneself and others, I was a *tabula rasa*—a blank slate. It took time and determination to gather knowledge and take action, but when I did, I freed myself from my limitations. First, I helped myself; then I began to help others.

Once I turned from fear to faith, I began to discover the transformation shifts and action steps needed to achieve success:

Step 1: Decide what you want and why.
Step 2: Change your glasses, change your life.

Step 3: Eliminate your limiting beliefs.

Step 4: Envision your outcome.

Step 5: Develop a plan.

Step 6: Banish distractions and focus.

Step 7: Take consistent action.

Step 8: Keep learning.

Step 9: Create a mission to give back.

As you'll see, with each simple (but not-so-easy) step, faith in yourself will grow. When you change how you think, then act, one success builds upon the other. Fear will lose its grip, and you will become the person you are meant to be.

It all begins with a shift in how you see yourself and your purpose—when you begin to see the possibilities. As Nelson Mandela once said, "It always seems impossible until it's done."

Miracles Are Everywhere

Numerous things happen on this planet that science can't explain: a mother lifts a car to save her child's life; a boy falls into an icy lake and is clinically dead for nearly an hour before coming back to life; people are healed despite official Western medicine declaring their diseases incurable; and so on. Just look at nature— mountains, valleys, animals, plants. Every day, the sun comes up; you may not see it if the sky is cloudy, yet the sun beams down and warms us.

Don't you think this is a miracle in and of itself?

But let me tell you the world's greatest miracle—a miracle no scientist or expert can fully explain or even replicate: you. You are the world's greatest miracle. Your existence evolved from an insignificantly tiny dot, from virtually nothing. When you were born, you were given an incredible gift. You didn't have to do anything to get it; the miracle of life was simply bestowed upon you. Cherish this miracle. Cherish your life and cherish yourself. The fact that you're breathing and that your heart is beating without you having to do anything, is nothing short of miraculous.

Because your life and the world around you are miraculous, have confidence that you possess the great resources and talents needed to make your vision and aspirations for yourself and your life a reality. Trust that you're capable; that you have far more potential within you than you have used or demonstrated up to this point.

You came to earth with a mission to complete. You didn't come here to blow out the candles on your birthday cake every year, only to be covered with dirt when your time is up. You didn't come to live someone else's life, only to fade into oblivion. You didn't come here to live a meaningless life. Nobody is born in this world without a purpose. Nobody is born a loser. Every individual carries a gift. Every individual deserves to live the life they choose. This includes you.

You came to this planet, to this world, to be happy. You came with a voice, music, a message, and an internal spark. You came here to give others everything you have to offer—to give them something good, something beautiful, and something useful for improving their lives. You came here to make this world a better place. In a thousand years, when you and I are gone, there will still be a trace written in the wind, the rain, and the sun, of someone who once lived on this planet and left a mark of love and determination, a mark of something beautiful, magnificent, and precious.

If you don't value yourself as the miracle that you are, you can't value others. If you don't value yourself as the miracle that you are, you won't be able to stand up for yourself; you won't be able to decide if you even deserve a breakthrough. If you don't value yourself as the miracle that you are, it will be difficult to help others . . . to live your purpose.

Not All Miracles Happen Overnight

Most people are waiting for a significant breakthrough. They're waiting for something big to happen—a burning bush to appear, the ability to walk on water, a winning lottery ticket. They're waiting for something that transforms their life overnight into what they desire. But all it really takes is a single small success that leads to your next move . . . which brings about your next success that leads to your next move. One on one, they build on the other.

Start with little things, and you will change your life.

For me, getting my health in order was just the beginning of my unlikely transformation. From there, all the other pieces of the puzzle clicked into place. My professional breakthrough was a logical result of breakthroughs I achieved in my personal life because the two arenas are intertwined.

This starting-small idea is well-known and used by people who experience breakthrough after breakthrough in their lives: when you achieve a breakthrough in one area of your life, all other areas will begin to improve.

Leonardo da Vinci, renowned for artistic masterpieces like the *Mona Lisa* and *The Last Supper*, went on to enjoy breakthroughs in scientific inquiry, where he made significant discoveries and advancements in fields ranging from anatomy to physics.

Marie Curie, a pioneering physicist and chemist who conducted groundbreaking research on radioactivity, earning her two Nobel Prizes in Physics and Chemistry, went on to become a prominent advocate for the use of radiation in medicine and founded the Curie Institutes in Paris and Warsaw, which continue to make significant contributions to cancer research and treatment.

Steve Jobs, co-founder of Apple Inc., played a crucial role in revolutionizing the technology industry with products like the iPhone, iPad, and MacBook. His breakthroughs in technology and design transformed multiple industries and made him one of the most influential entrepreneurs of the modern era. Additionally, Jobs experienced personal growth and breakthroughs in his approach to leadership and creativity throughout his career, as evidenced by his return to Apple in the late 1990s and the subsequent development of innovative products.

Oprah Winfrey initially gained fame as a television host and media mogul, hosting *The Oprah Winfrey Show*, which became one of the highest-rated talk shows in television history. Through her platform, Winfrey achieved breakthroughs in communication, storytelling, and empowerment. She later expanded her influence into various other areas, including publishing, film production, philanthropy, and advocacy for social causes, experiencing breakthroughs in each domain.

These examples demonstrate how individuals who achieve breakthroughs in one area of their lives often possess qualities and skills that enable them to succeed in multiple areas, leveraging their initial successes to drive further innovation and growth.

Focus on one area first, with all your heart and might, and you will achieve your breakthrough in that area. You'll be amazed how other areas start to improve too, and you'll be equipped with new experiences to help you achieve new breakthroughs. You'll be blown away by the results.

Your Emotional State Matters

Your small wins and growing faith in yourself will help you develop a healthy emotional state for the journey ahead. This will help you stay on the course when you encounter challenges.

A healthy emotional state encompasses a range of positive emotions and coping mechanisms that enable you to navigate these challenges effectively. A healthy emotional state is comprised of . . .

1. **Emotional awareness:** being aware of and acknowledging your emotions without judgment, which allows for better self-regulation and communication.

2. **Resilience:** bouncing back from adversity and setbacks; coping with stress, adapting to change, and maintaining a positive outlook despite challenges.

3. **Emotional regulation:** managing both positive and negative feelings in a balanced way, recognizing triggers, employing coping strategies, and maintaining emotional stability.

4. **Self-compassion:** being kind and understanding toward yourself, acknowledging your flaws and mistakes without harsh self-criticism.

5. **Adaptability:** being open to change, willing to learn from experiences, and adjusting your expectations and behaviors as needed to contribute to overall well-being.

6. **Sense of purpose:** finding deep meaning in life, engaging in activities that align with your values and goals for both fulfillment and contentment.

7. **Healthy coping mechanisms:** using constructive coping strategies to manage stress and difficult emotions. These may include exercise, mindfulness, creative expression, seeking social support, or seeking professional help when needed.

8. **Boundaries:** setting limits on others' behavior and respecting your own needs.

9. **Joy and gratitude**: embracing moments of joy and practicing gratitude for life's blessings, cultivating positive emotions, and savoring life's pleasures.

Overall, a healthy emotional state will enable you to navigate life's ups and downs with greater ease and satisfaction. And there will be ups and downs. This should come as no surprise.

The Opposite of a Healthy Emotional State

In the past, I repeatedly questioned myself when I ran into a challenge. *Why is this happening to me? Why now? What did I do wrong? When will this end?* I had a whole litany I would take myself through, which left me feeling helpless. Then I realized that none of *this*, whatever *this* was, was happening *to* me, but *for* me. It happened for me to finally wake up and realize I was not living the life I wanted to live—which was the precursor to a breakthrough.

Those questions were evidence of my victim mentality, the killer of positive feelings.

If you believe one wrong move equals failure, that *you* are a failure, that you could not possibly get anywhere, and no one could blame you for playing small and staying safe. Take on this victim mentality right from the start before we get to the mindset-shifting part of this process.

Who you are and what you do are not the same things. Your value isn't represented by the figures in your bank account or by your degree. You're a miracle, don't you forget that. Don't indulge in self-pity. Don't play the victim to win people's sympathy or support. You will make your current situation even worse. Avoid blaming others for your failures. You've had them before; you'll have more. Don't hold other people responsible for your actions or your failure to progress. If you want to move faster towards your dreams and goals, put yourself in a good emotional state. The only person who has the power, the freedom, and the capacity to create a breakthrough in your life is you. You are responsible for your life. Other people are accountable for their lives and their own breakthroughs. That's called boundaries.

"But I'm not playing the victim," you may say. And while it may not be as obvious as that woman who showed up at my workshop, we all play the victim from time to time. Even now, I catch myself occasionally falling into a victim mindset. It is the most useless attitude a person can have. It serves neither you nor those around you and prevents you from getting the results you desire in life. Commit to losing it right now.

Take the First Step

If, after reading this book, you take only one action, make it this one: assume responsibility and start your life afresh, without making excuses or playing the victim. Be done with that; relegate that approach to the past.

What matters is that you want to better something in your life, and you have a roadmap in front of you made up of doable action steps. By itself, this roadmap isn't worth anything if you don't follow it, step by step. Only by acting will you enjoy the outcomes you desire.

Follow the directions and you will achieve what you desire, get where you want to be. Take it one small step at a time and you will liberate yourself once and for all. You will live up to the potential you know is inside you and achieve far more than you ever thought possible.

Start today. Right now—this is the ideal moment to get started; not tomorrow, or the day after tomorrow—*now*. It doesn't matter how old you are; in any event, your time is limited, so don't wait to start making changes. Achieve your breakthrough.

The world needs you.

Switching your mindset from "I think I can" to "I'm going to make it happen" is a game changer.

2

DECIDE WHAT YOU WANT AND WHY

Those who have a "why" to live, can bear with almost any "how."
—**Viktor Frankl**

Oftentimes, people go around in circles, seeking excuses not to make a breakthrough. Because of past decisions, they accept their justifications as facts and predictors of their future. Or they think of some impossible goal that cannot be achieved under any circumstances due to inherent contradictions, violations of physical laws, or logical impossibilities, and decide that all goals are therefore useless.

Unfortunately, if you play this head game, you'll dismiss your potential and the fantastic results you can achieve.

You can accomplish a breakthrough in every area of your life, regardless of your restrictions or excuses. You can go from the couch to the marathon finish line in a matter of months. You can find your soulmate, fix your marriage, create a lasting connection with your child, find a new position, make more money—and your breakthrough can begin immediately.

How do you accomplish this? You use the power of choice, the power of intention which is already inside you. In other words, you direct your thoughts and behavior toward what you desire, and you do so with determination. Your big breakthrough starts with a single decision.

Deciding Is the First Step to Breaking Free

Make a choice to commit, to achieve your outcome by a specific date. (Remember, a goal without a deadline is just a dream.) The power of intention—"I have decided this is the way it will be"—is crucial to your breakthrough; it is the driving force behind your actions and decisions. Switching your mindset from *I think I can* to *I will make it happen* is a game changer. Intention helps clarify what you want to achieve and directs your focus.

Clear intentions may sound like:

I will lose fifty pounds so I can feel alive in my body by December 31.

I will lose fifty pounds so I can feel alive in my body by December 31.

I will get my PhD by the end of the fall semester of 2025.

I will communicate with my spouse each day in such a way that we fall in love all over again.

I will double my income in the next calendar year.

I will become CEO of the company before I turn thirty.

I will create a social network of diehard friends by the end of this summer.

When you set clear intentions that are date specific, you are far more likely to align your actions and efforts with those goals, increasing your chances of success. When you have a strong intention to achieve a specific thing, you are more likely to stay dedicated and persevere in the face of obstacles or setbacks.

Intention helps cultivate a positive mindset by fostering belief in your ability to achieve your goals. When you set positive intentions and affirm your capabilities, you create a supportive mental environment that enhances your confidence and resilience. Intention serves as a precursor to visualization and manifestation, which we'll get to soon enough. By clearly defining your intentions, you can better visualize yourself achieving your goals, which can activate the unconscious mind and attract opportunities and resources that align with your intentions.

Intention helps focus your energy and resources on what truly matters to you, preventing distractions and inefficiencies that can derail your progress. You'll allocate your time and effort more effectively and generate momentum by initiating action and progress toward your goals, thereby propelling you forward.

Make a definitive, firm, and unwavering *decision*, with no option of going back. Decide now to make a breakthrough. Decide now on a new life. Decide on who you want to become. Decide now that you'll no longer accept or put up with what you don't deserve. You're deserving of so much more and you're more worthy than you realize. So, clench your fists and affirm you'll create a breakthrough.

Put Yourself in a Good Emotional State

As we touched on earlier, when you think differently, when you trust and come from a good emotional state, your new behavior will produce new results. You will continue to improve your behavior until you get the results you want.

Once a decision is made, you need to be aware and acknowledge your emotions without judgment. This will help solidify your sense of purpose. You'll be better able to bounce back from adversity and setbacks, manage both positive and negative feelings in a balanced way, and have some level of constructive coping strategy, self-compassion, and adaptability.

If this sounds challenging given your current state, don't worry. For now, simply remember that you have it within your power to put yourself in a good emotional state and make good judgments. Adjust your posture and focus your attention on what you're capable of doing right now.

To start, ask better questions. Better questions provide better answers and will assist you in maintaining a positive emotional state. For example, when you can't seem to get off the couch and go for a run when you know you should, you could ask yourself, *why am I such a loser?* But that will do nothing for your emotional state except bring it down. Instead, you could ask yourself, *how could I anchor in the new behavior of running after work?* That question sparks ideas: you could put your running shoes by the front entrance of your home to remind you of your task; park down the street and cover the extra distance on foot, regularly take a run before you allow yourself to enter your front door. Notice the difference.

Consider using affirmations and mantras as well. Mantras and affirmations are helpful in goal achievement for several reasons. They affirm desired outcomes and reinforce the belief in your ability to achieve goals. They can counteract your negative self-talk and doubts and help you maintain a confident and optimistic mindset. When you articulate goals in concise, affirmative statements, you clarify your intentions and direct your attention toward specific outcomes. In doing so, you increase your motivation and commit to achieving them. Mantras and affirmations have the potential to program your mind for success. When you consistently repeat positive statements, you embed messages into your unconscious mind, influencing your beliefs, attitudes, and behaviors to align with your goals.

Repeat the following words in your head, out loud, as you walk or drive. Repeat them anywhere, with determination: "I will reach a breakthrough! I will reach a breakthrough! I'm deciding on a breakthrough and on a new, different life because ... [fill-in-the-blank]."

One more thing: you'll find sample affirmations and mantras at https://aleksandersinigoj.com/victor.

EXERCISE: Choose Your Focus

Take a piece of paper and write down:

1.   The area I want to achieve my first breakthrough:

2.   My goal:

Now, repeat your goal aloud or in your mind several times a day.

Your Goal, Not Someone Else's

To increase the possibility of massive success, the breakthrough you set out to achieve should belong to you, otherwise, your accomplishments may be short-lasting or unfulfilling. Take other people out of the equation.

Your desires are deeply personal, yet they are often confused by outside influence. It is not necessary to compare yourself to others (though many of us often do), neither is it necessary to prove yourself to others or impress them.

You should be the one reason for making that breakthrough. Make this breakthrough because *you* desire to achieve it. Make this breakthrough because *you* want to accomplish something. It doesn't really matter what breakthrough your neighbor may have had. It doesn't even matter what your neighbor accomplished. It doesn't matter what others think or do. You must choose your own path.

Again, I repeat, this is your life. As your life, you can modify and tailor it to suit your own desires, aspirations, and objectives. Let others have their dreams. At the same time, pick the dreams that inspire *you*.

Don't confine this one life to the ideas and aspirations of other people. The mere thought—that you're leading the life you choose—can make it fabulous, magnificent, and powerful.

Your Why

I've helped thousands and thousands of individuals from all over the world make various life breakthroughs. What I've found is that it's not about their ability. It's all about motivation, or the "why:" why do you (or don't you) want to achieve this breakthrough? When you know your "why," you've got your because. I do this because . . .

One of the most powerful motivations for goal achievement is to connect with your "why."

Think about it. Would you donate your heart—your liver, your lungs—to save the life of your child? Would you give your life for the sake of your child or another loved one? Of course, you would. If your "why" is big enough, you would sacrifice anything; you would move mountains, all in the interest of achieving the outcome.

One of my favorite authors, Anthony de Mello, tells a story that never fails to inspire; it goes like this . . .

A little girl was dying of an illness from which her eight-year-old brother had recovered some time before. The doctor said to the boy, "Only a transfusion of your blood can save the life of your sister. Are you willing to donate your blood?"

The boy's eyes widened in fear. He hesitated for a moment and then said, "All right, doctor, I'll do it." An hour after the blood transfusion, the young boy hesitantly asked the doctor, "How soon until I start to die?"

It wasn't until that moment that the doctor realized why the boy was terrified. The little boy had thought that with his blood donation, he would be literally giving his life to save his sister's.

Your most powerful "why" is something that is greater than yourself. Frequently, it's linked to unconditional love: love for a child, a parent, a spouse, an animal, nature, the planet, your country, God, life. Yet, your "why" might also be a desire for change and a better life for yourself and those you care about.

How quickly could you make a breakthrough in your profession, finances, or health, if it meant saving your child's life? Could you make one million dollars in a short period of time in a fair and ethical way? Could you stop smoking? Could you reach your ideal weight? I bet you could.

When I asked thousands and thousands of individuals around the world this question, the response was almost invariably yes. Why? Because they'd discovered something far more valuable than they could possibly conceive of or comprehend. When you uncover your "why," you'll do whatever it takes. Suddenly, something that previously seemed impossible, even unthinkable, becomes straightforward and nonnegotiable.

Other Driving Forces

Your breakthrough may be driven by a variety of motivations, which can vary depending on your nature, your circumstances, and the kind of goals themselves. Short of unconditional love, your "why" might be motivation in the shape of a carrot or a stick, pleasure or pain, positive or negative.

Some common motivations or drivers behind goal achievement include...

1. Intrinsic motivation

This type of motivation arises from internal factors, such as personal satisfaction, enjoyment, or a sense of fulfillment derived from achieving the goal itself. Intrinsic motivation often leads to sustained effort and engagement because individuals are driven by their inherent interest or passion for the activity or outcome.

2. Extrinsic rewards

External rewards, such as financial incentives, recognition, or praise, can motivate individuals to pursue and achieve goals. These rewards provide tangible benefits or acknowledgments for their efforts, serving as external reinforcement for goal-directed behavior.

3. Personal growth and development

Many people are motivated to achieve goals as a means of personal growth and self-improvement. They seek to expand their knowledge, skills, or capabilities and view goal achievement as a pathway to self-actualization and realizing their full potential.

4. Social connection and approval

Human beings are social creatures, and the desire for social connection, acceptance, and approval can be powerful motivators for goal achievement. Individuals may pursue goals to gain recognition, respect, or acceptance from others, or to fulfill societal expectations and norms.

5. Sense of purpose or meaning

Goals that align with an individual's values, beliefs, or sense of purpose can be deeply motivating. When people feel connected to a higher purpose or mission, they are more likely to be driven by a sense of meaning and significance in their pursuit of goals.

6. Desire for autonomy and control

Some individuals are motivated by the desire for autonomy and control over their lives. They seek to set and achieve goals that enable them to make independent decisions, exercise agency, and shape their own destiny.

7. Fear of failure or consequences

Fear can be a powerful motivator for goal achievement, particularly when individuals perceive the consequences of failure as significant or undesirable. The fear of failure may drive individuals to exert extra effort, persevere in the face of challenges, or take calculated risks to avoid negative outcomes.

8. Competitiveness or achievement orientation

Some people are inherently driven by a desire to excel, compete, or outperform others. They thrive on the challenge of setting ambitious goals and surpassing benchmarks, viewing achievement as a measure of their success and competence.

These motivations interact and overlap in complex ways, but they help shape behaviors, attitudes, and persistence in pursuing goals. If you can understand and harness these motivations, you can increase your success in achieving your breakthrough.

Let Your Why Carry You the Distance

Many individuals give up because they're daunted by not knowing "how" to achieve a breakthrough. When you have your true "why," you'll notice a path appearing in front of you—your "how"—which I will expound upon further as we go along.

That is why it's so important that you *decide* and have a strong enough "why." You're capable of doing anything, even if it looks impossible right now. You might become a multimillionaire in a matter of months, you might become enormously successful in your career, lose weight, or work out every day for several hours . . . anything you want.

When you discover your true "why" and respond with "because" you'll be able to achieve a life-changing breakthrough. Your answer is concealed within the key word "why." Constantly look for reasons that will help you make a breakthrough rather than those that won't. Never stop seeking for your "why;" never stop refining it and using it to strengthen your decision to reach a breakthrough. It's what will carry you the distance.

EXERCISE: Your Why

Answer the questions below; they are the reasons for (and the driving force behind) your breakthrough—they are your "why." Your answers will encourage you to stay on track and remind you of why you want to make a breakthrough. Respond honestly about how you feel in the moment.

1. Why do I want to achieve a breakthrough?
2. What will I receive when I achieve a breakthrough?
3. Who else will benefit when I achieve a breakthrough?
4. What impact will a breakthrough have on my life and the lives of others?

Now write down your decision and commitment to making a breakthrough.

Whenever someone asks you if anything is possible, always say yes. Because it is possible. Maybe you don't know how to accomplish it yet, whatever *it* is for you. Maybe no one else in the world has done it before or knows how to do it yet. Remember, the world changes rapidly. What we thought was impossible yesterday is now reality, so what is impossible today will be feasible tomorrow.

The obstacle lies in your inner world—in your model of the world.

3

CHANGE YOUR GLASSES, CHANGE YOUR LIFE

———

It's during our darkest moments that we must focus to see the light.
–Aristotle Onassis

We humans live in two worlds: the internal world and the external world. A breakthrough happens first in your internal world. When you change on the inside, your life will also change on the outside. When both worlds are reconciled the breakthrough can happen even faster.

Your external world contains everything you desire in life: health, family, relationships, partnership, career, money, and happiness. (If I missed something, simply add it to the list.) Your inner world is made up of values, beliefs, strategies, anchors, behavior, and experience, the sum of which represents your identity and how you see yourself.

You might say your inner world is your model of the world. This is your comprehensive understanding of reality that accounts for the intricate, interconnected, and often nonlinear relationships between various factors, variables, and systems. It's sophisticated and nuanced; it acknowledges that things are rarely governed by simple, linear cause-and-effect relationships. Instead, it considers the emergence of patterns, feedback loops, emergent properties, and nonlinearity, which can lead to unexpected outcomes and behaviors.

Your model of the world is essentially the lens, the filter, through which you view life. It is unique to you, which means expecting other people to consistently share your views or see a situation as you do is pointless because they see the world through an entirely different pair of glasses.

Some people wear rose-tinted glasses, others wear dark shades, others still peer through lenses that are constantly smeary. Whatever your lens, it represents your limited view of the world and life.

You can live with this limited view for years, even decades, believing in things that aren't necessarily true or relevant simply because you can't see things any differently. Then one day you put on a new pair of glasses with lenses that provide a better, more accurate picture. It's then you realize what's what. This is the experience that people often refer to as a "breakthrough." It's a shift in your understanding of the world and your way of thinking. All other breakthroughs flow from there.

Your Inner World Is the Obstacle

Don't blame the external world when you don't get what you want in life. It's not someone else's fault; it's not the fault of your unfortunate situation, where you were born, or the color of your hair. Motivational speaker Nick Vujicic was born without arms and legs, yet he continues to live life to the fullest. He has a family; he enjoys skiing and swimming; he gives talks and inspires people all over the world. He is a prime example of someone who overcame external challenges.

Obstacles lie in your inner world—in your model of the world. This is what hinders you from achieving whatever you seek in life. It is your view of your past experiences, yourself, and the world at large that restricts your ability to manifest the money you desire, or pursue the job, healthy relationships, powerful partnerships you desire, and so on.

If you want to grow in life and for some reason you don't grow, your model of the world might be your greatest obstacle. If you're an entrepreneur and you just can't seem to make it, your model of the world might be the biggest hindrance to the success of your business. Likewise, your model of the world—which determines how you view events and react to each situation—can limit your love relationship. You must understand that there are no opponents and no limitations on the outside. These exist only within you.

By changing your lenses, you change your model of the world. When you change your beliefs (and you can)—when you create new anchors, begin using new strategies, and redefine yourself-you will begin to see the impact in your life. As if by magic, you attain more money, a better career, deeper relationships, remarkable health, spiritual growth . . . whatever else you desire in life. Luck is now yours. Before you can change your model of the world, it helps to understand the focal points. They include values, beliefs, experiences, strategies, anchors, behaviors, and identity.

1. Values

Our values are governed by our model of the world. They tend to be enduring and stable over time, reflecting deep-seated beliefs about what is right or wrong, good or bad; they represent core principles and ideals that guide behavior and decision-making by serving as criteria for evaluating choices and actions. Honesty, integrity, compassion, fairness, justice, loyalty, respect, personal growth—whatever our values, they represent what we consider desirable, worthwhile, or morally significant.

We each have two types of values: theoretical values (what we think we value) and practical values (how we actually spend our money, time, and energy—proving what we truly value). For example, if you say family is the most important value in your life, yet you choose work over spending time with them, family is your theoretical value, work is your practical value. Many times, people say health is their most important value, and yet they fail to eat fresh unprocessed foods, exercise, sleep well, etc. They only say that something is important, but they don't do it, that is the main difference between theoretical and practical values. If you don't know what your values are, simply look at how you spend your time and other resources. This will help you separate the theoretical from the practical.

Oftentimes, values conflict with each other. You might want a successful career that requires you to take risks to succeed, but you also want safety. That inner struggle between values can be a significant obstacle to creating a breakthrough and accomplishing the objective you want to achieve because your values also have their own hierarchy, or order in which they are ranked.

Your hierarchy of values shapes your beliefs, strategies, and behaviors (only after considering the highest ranked value, do you consider the second, third, fourth, and so on). As such, it impacts the outcomes you obtain in life, making it one of the most significant components of your model of the world. And this order is constantly changing. What was important to you as a child or teenager may not be as important to you today. Some of the things that were at the top of your value hierarchy then are no longer relevant today.

To have success with the changes you want to make in your life, you need to have a clear hierarchy of values. Let's say you want to become a coach so you can help others. It would be helpful if you valued entrepreneurship and being self-employed, more than you value security. Why? Because this choice requires you to deal with the regular ups and downs that are part of building a business: there's no regular paycheck; there's no one but yourself to keep you accountable; there's no safety net, which may lead to criticism from others. If your values don't align, you will not act, you will not move forward towards your stated goal.

Exercise: Your Current Value Hierarchy

To figure out the current value hierarchy at play:

1. List your values.

2. Order them from most to least important.

3. Look for potential conflicts.

4. Which values do you need to change so you can achieve your stated goal? Connect the end result to your hierarchy of values because if you don't have the most important part of your inner world supporting you, nothing will happen.

Of course, shifting the order of your values requires some force. One way to go about it is to create a sense of urgency. When you think you have time, you are far more likely to postpone change—to offer a whole host of objections or a litany of limiting beliefs.

To create that urgency, you basically connect a value—whether one you need to change or one you need to own—to pain or pleasure.

Think of it this way, you may want to live a healthy lifestyle . . . but you're young; you're too tired to work out at the end of the day; your comfort food tastes too good. You'll try again next week—until you're hit with a health crisis. Once your health (or lack thereof) causes pain, you are much more likely to change. When you look into the future and imagine the pain associated with not changing your value system, you create that same sense of urgency, without actually "going there."

2. Beliefs

While values are what you think is important, beliefs are what you think is true. Beliefs are specific thoughts or convictions about the nature of reality that influence perceptions and inter-pretations. They are often based on personal experiences, cul-tural influences, or social conditioning. They can also vary in strength and flexibility, ranging from deeply held convictions to more tentative opinions or hypotheses.

You first acquired your beliefs from your parents, who needed to set certain boundaries in order for you to thrive and survive in this world. Then there were your teachers, classmates and friends, physicians, and so on. Everyone you have encountered has contrib-uted in some way to your beliefs, whether you recognize it or not.

It is important to understand that you are not the victim of your beliefs. You can choose what to believe. Due to circum-stances in your life, you may have been told what to believe in the past; you may have created beliefs that served you at the time.

In other words, you chose to believe something then. So, you can choose to believe something that can serve you better now.

Take my old choirmaster, for instance. When I was twelve years old, my choirmaster told me to stop singing because I sounded like a bear. From that point on, I had the belief that when I opened my mouth, I growled like a grizzly, even though we have only brown bears in Slovenia. To date, I've recorded hundreds of hours of audio and video content, never once sounding like either type of bear, which dispels that theory. Yet, it took me way too long to lose that belief because I didn't have the right tools.

Certain beliefs help you achieve your goals; others hamper you. The latter are known as limiting beliefs. Your limiting beliefs are an impediment to reaching your goals. For example, if you base your identity, sense of self, ego, self-worth, self-esteem on being right, admitting you were wrong is a major threat. Whereas, if you base your world view on getting it right—valuing curiosity and a lifetime of learning—changing your mind is a moment of growth.

I'll expound more in the next chapter. For now, you need only know that having limiting beliefs in the area where you wish to attain a goal is like hitting the gas and brake pedals at the same time. Your car will stay put.

Be more like a child, without limitations; strive to believe anything is possible.

3. Experiences

Your history can be a burden or an opportunity; it can be a punishment or a blessing. What you may not know is that you have a choice in how you perceive your personal experiences and the meaning you give them.

People frequently make the mistake of not allowing themselves to dream big because of their fears and limitations. They look at previous experiences and they are afraid ... so their aspirations go no further.

People who've been in a terrible relationship in the past frequently carry this pain into a new relationship. They're unlikely to imagine having one that's healthy, long-lasting, and joyful. They're afraid to envision something beautiful and optimistic. They keep playing old films in their head and remembering past images of unpleasant experiences from one or more relationships. As a result, they lose sight of the path they're on and program their future with a fear of the past repeating itself.

Even when they think and dream about abundance, people who have experienced financial issues in the past can't "sense" it. When they visualize the desired goal, they don't see themselves at the finish line; they imagine an unhappy ending. And what do they get? They get what they've imagined and felt. This is how they throw barriers in their own way, preventing them from realizing their dreams and goals. They rationalize their actions by stating, "I'm realistic. I'm not a dreamer."

Yet I have been moved, moved to tears, by people who were subjected to all kinds of limitations and abuse, in environments with no opportunities, who still managed to find the strength and energy to get back on their feet and create beautiful, happy, and successful lives. They live on their own terms and are the masters of their own fate.

More and more I realize that where you come from doesn't really matter when it comes to achieving a breakthrough. It makes no difference what occurred in your past. It is your model of the world that makes all the difference. You have the option to view the world differently than you do today. You can move from victim to victor with one simple decision, with one simple belief. Regardless of what you've experienced or gone through in the past, you can change your perception of it. Will you?

Your experiences are film clips that can be interpreted in any number of ways. Choose a better interpretation.

4. Strategies, Anchors, and Behaviors

We each have internal factors that influence our thoughts, emotions, and decision making. They make up predictable internal strategies that anchor how we act and respond to events in life and our overall behavior.

Internal strategies rely on what you've learned, connecting past events, beliefs, values, and cultural norms. How you write the letter "A" is a simple strategy stored in your inner world. You always write it in the same manner. How you eat, how you dress, how you compose letters—all of these strategies are predictable and unconscious competencies.

Internal strategies also direct your emotions and how you cope with external stimuli. They may include mindfulness, relaxation techniques, or reframing negative thoughts to manage stress, anxiety, or other emotional challenges. Unfortunately, not all coping strategies are healthy. Drinking, self-isolation, and finger-pointing are three prime examples.

Since internal strategies build upon past experiences, they create decision-making shortcuts to help you make decisions quickly and efficiently. These shortcuts are often based on standards or cognitive biases, relying on initial information or information readily available.

They become something of an anchor, keeping you in place, ensuring you always respond to a certain event in a specific way. It's predictable. You have hundreds and hundreds of anchors. Some produce a positive emotional state (how you react to your favorite song); others produce a negative emotional state.

Negative anchors can be formed in any number of ways. Let's say as a child you were asked to step in front of the classroom to perform a song; when you did, your classmates laughed at you.

Problems arise when you rely on anchors and strategies that are ineffective for you and take you away from your objectives. Using the example above, if I put you in front of an audience, but you're afraid of public speaking (due to the anchor from your childhood), your reaction will be predictable: terror.

You can carry anchors within you for decades. I met one student whose father had horrible money problems. He filed for bankruptcy, and a continuous stream of debt collectors rang their bell at all hours, day and night. They were so aggressive that they would try to force their way in the door. Though young at the time, the student continued to carry the fear anchored in that experience. The mere sound of a doorbell would send her into a fit of rage—she refused to have one on her door.

Thankfully, negative anchors can be replaced. You can heal from even the most traumatic experiences and incidents. Through learning and adjusting your behavior based on feedback and experiences, you can develop new strategies. Through trial and error, you can refine your internal strategies and anchors, adapting them to new situations and circumstances to optimize your behavior and outcomes.

It's what I teach in one of my workshops—how to develop new anchors and replace negative ones in order to achieve a breakthrough. It's what I taught that student anchored to a fear of doorbells: collapse the not-so-useful old anchor; delete what's no longer useful, and replace it with a positive and powerful one.

It starts with a few questions:

How would it feel now if . . . ?

Have I ever felt this before in my life?

Can I imagine experiencing this in the future?

Then, you anchor that imagined state to something you do (either internal or external), pumping your fist in the air, for example. Exclaiming, "You've got this!" Envisioning bright lights on a stage. And with the use of past, existing, and future states, you develop a new, more powerful anchor—one that holds you to your goals.

Again, make sure you get all the extra training videos and resources that go along with this book, including an anchor-development training. https://aleksandersinigoj.com/victor.

5. Identity

The last (but not least) important dimension of our inner world is our identity, or how we define ourselves. Most people believe their identity is fixed, but that is not true. Believing that your identity is fixed can interfere with your big breakthrough in several ways. When you strongly identify with a particular self-image or identity, you may resist changes that are necessary to achieve your goals. For example, if you identify as someone who doesn't take risks, pursuing a goal that requires risk-taking might be a challenge because it conflicts with your self-perception.

Your identity also shapes your beliefs about what you can and cannot do. If your identity includes beliefs like "I'm not good at public speaking" or "I'm not a creative person," these beliefs can limit your willingness to try new things or develop skills necessary for achieving your goals. Wealthy people whose identity is to be wealthy regain their money even if they lose it because being wealthy is part of who they are, their identity.

If you strongly identify with being successful or competent in a certain way, it is very likely that you will do all that you can to live up to that identity, which means that you will be learning, improving, growing, and becoming who you think you are. If your identity is to be a health-conscious individual, you will most likely prioritize your well-being and make informed choices about your diet and physical activity, which means you will not need a diet to achieve your fitness goal, this will be your lifestyle, your way of living because it is part of your identity.

Those very same goals often require adaptability and sometimes even a change in approach. If your identity is rigid, you may struggle to adapt to new circumstances or feedback, which are crucial for making progress towards your goals. Clinging to a specific identity can also blind you to opportunities that don't align with that identity. You may overlook chances for growth or success because they don't fit with your preconceived notions of who you are or what you're capable of.

To mitigate these challenges, it's important to cultivate a growth mindset where you see your identity as flexible and evolving over time in response to various internal and external influences. Recognize as well that your identity has many distinct parts.

- Your **personal identity** encompasses your unique personality, traits, experiences, and individual history. This includes your interests, talents, preferences, strengths, weaknesses, and personal achievements. Personal identity reflects who you see yourself as, an individual separate from others.

- **Social identity** refers to the aspects of identity that are shaped by your membership in various social groups, categories, or communities. This includes race, ethnicity, gender, sexual orientation, religion, nationality, socioeconomic status, and occupation. Social identity provides you with a sense of belonging and connection to broader social contexts.

- Your **cultural identity** encompasses the beliefs, values, traditions, customs, language, and cultural practices that you inherit or adopt from your cultural background or heritage. It reflects the shared norms and values of a particular cultural group and shapes how you perceive yourself in relation to your cultural community.

- **Role identity** refers to the roles and positions you occupy in your social interactions and relationships. This includes the role of parent, child, sibling, friend, student, employee, entrepreneur, leader, or caregiver. Role identity influences your behavior and expectations within specific social contexts and relationships.

- **Professional identity** encompasses the roles, responsibilities, skills, qualifications, and values associated with your occupation or career. This includes job title, professional affiliations, expertise, achievements, and career aspirations. Your professional identity influences how you perceive yourself in the workplace and interact with colleagues and clients.

- **Interpersonal identity** refers to the roles and relationships you establish and maintain with others in your social networks. This includes friendships, romantic relationships, family dynamics, and social connections.

As you can see, identity is a multifaceted and complex construct that integrates various personal, social, cultural, and contextual factors. It provides you with a sense of self-awareness, continuity, and belonging, shaping your sense of purpose, meaning, and direction in life.

But there's one aspect of identity I suggest you walk away from right this minute—that of victim.

When you play the victim, you keep yourself in a negative state of vibration and emotion that prevents you from obtaining what you want. When you play the victim, you're walking away from your objective rather than towards it. Instead of receiving what you desire, you move away from it. If you want to get what you want, start accepting responsibility for your life and stop making excuses. Stop creating excuses, since they serve no purpose other than to program your mind for failure and keep you from achieving your goals. Whatever you claim you can't do, that's unfeasible, there's someone in the world who has done it despite limitations. Choose to be that someone.

We'll cover how to do that in the next chapter.

For now, take some time to refocus . . .

EXERCISE: Identify Your Values, Strategies, and Behaviors

Clean up:

1. Write down all your values that influence or govern the selected area of your life, the ones that currently limit you.

2. Which strategies and behaviors aren't working for you and are taking you away from your objectives?

Get clear:

1. Write down all the resources (for example, your values, strategies, and behaviors, such as courage, persistence, experiences, etc.) that you already have and that are assisting you on your way to a breakthrough.

Seek:

1. Which new, helpful values do you need to achieve a breakthrough?

2. Which new, helpful strategies and behaviors do you need to achieve a breakthrough?

3. Who would you like to become? What is your desired identity that will propel you to success?

You must first achieve
victory in your thoughts
before you can achieve
it in reality.

4

ELIMINATE YOUR LIMITING BELIEFS

---

*Personal growth is not a matter of learning new information
but of unlearning old limits.*
–Alan Cohen

L imiting beliefs are deeply ingrained convictions or assumptions that you hold about yourself, others, or the world around you, which constrain your perceptions, actions, and potential. These beliefs typically stem from past experiences, cultural influences, societal norms, or internalized messages, and they often serve to undermine your confidence, create self-doubt, and restrict your personal growth and fulfillment. This is why when you change your thoughts, you change your actions. This is why you must first achieve victory in your thoughts before you can achieve it in reality.

As I've said, I live in a small, beautiful country on the sunny side of the Alps, Slovenia. Slovenia is a beautiful country; I could never imagine abandoning it, no matter how high I rise or how many countries I visit and immediately feel at home. As with any culture, the history, social norms, and cultural values of Slovenia have influenced my limiting beliefs and those of my countrymen. Of course, within any society, there is a wide range of beliefs influenced by various factors, including personal experiences, upbringing, and so on, but there are certain themes or patterns more prevalent due to historical context.

Because Slovenia has experienced significant political and economic upheaval throughout its history, including periods of foreign rule, conflict, and economic uncertainty, some Slovenians hold a belief that stability and security are fleeting, leading to a fear of taking risks or pursuing ambitious goals. Slovenia has also faced challenges related to authoritarian rule and oppression, particularly during periods of foreign domination.

This history has contributed to a general mistrust of authority figures or institutions, leading to skepticism towards government, corporations, or other forms of authority. The experiences of World War II instilled a survival mentality among some Slovenians, leading to beliefs such as "you can't rely on anyone but yourself" or "life is a struggle." This mindset often leads to a focus on self-reliance and independence, but it can also hinder collaboration and trust-building in relationships.

Economic instability, limited resources, and geopolitical challenges lead some Slovenians to believe that opportunities for success and advancement are scarce or inaccessible. This belief can discourage ambition or risk-taking behavior, leading to a sense of resignation or complacency. All these beliefs can be changed.

People succeed despite their current circumstances all the time, proving them wrong.

Regardless of your nationality, you can see why overcoming limiting beliefs—of recognizing and challenging ingrained patterns of thinking, reframing negative self-talk, and cultivating a mindset of empowerment, resilience, and self-compassion—is so important.

The fundamental question is whether your model of the world, your inner world, allows you to live the life you want to live. If you want to unlock your potential and pursue your goals with confidence and determination, you need to take a good hard look at your limiting beliefs and make sure they are not holding you back.

Take an Inventory of Your Limiting Beliefs

Most of your limiting beliefs are useless. Perhaps you acquired them when you were younger. Perhaps they're the product of how you were raised. Perhaps they were useful at some point in your life. But if they're now preventing you from attaining your objectives, it's time to change or discard them.

Before you can accomplish this task, you need to know which beliefs hinder you. You need to take inventory; once you write them down, you can see which ones hold you back.

Some limiting beliefs will be obvious:

I'm not worth it, and I don't deserve this.

I'll never make it.

Who do I think I am, believing that I'll be successful?

I don't have the necessary education.

Some may be harder to spot. To get the juices flowing, here are a few examples from some of my workshop participants. These were the reasons they weren't getting the money, career, relationships, and so on that they wanted.

1. Money Beliefs

If you want to become rich but have a limiting belief about money (money is bad; all rich people are thieves) your money getting strategies and behaviors will be useless because your unconscious mind rejects money.

Martin (or so we'll call him) wanted nothing more than to be financially successful, yet he was as far away from that reality as he could get. Clearly, he held limiting views about money and finances. The goal was to uncover what they were, so he could change or replace them with new, more useful ones.

Remember, every belief we hold is a decision. If you choose to believe something at some point in your life, but this idea no longer serves you, you can change your mind.

"But money isn't that important to me anyway," Martin said.

This, by the way, is how many people think and talk about money because they gave up long ago. Rather than battle for what they want and persevere, they give up—then comfort themselves or attempt to convince themselves that they don't want or need it. And that is precisely the reason they're unable to achieve the financial goals set for themselves. Martin is not alone; it happens to countless others ... perhaps it's happened to you.

Martin also believed that he had to work hard (instead of smart) to get money. He believed the only way to make a living was to exchange his time for money. Having the victim mentality made him believe that he was a victim of current circumstances. As a result, the number of hours worked determined his earnings. He acknowledged that time on this planet is limited; we only have twenty-four hours in a day; the amount he could work was restricted. He conceded that there are numerous completely legal ways to avoid the traditional time-for-money exchange; the digital world and new technologies make this possible today. He could see that the more value he provided to as many people as possible, the more money he would earn in return.

To further shift his belief system, I brought up the nature of money and what it is meant to do for each of us.

Money comes in various forms, and there have never been more opportunities to earn money than now. Money is vital in the world we live in because it serves as a medium for the exchange of goods and services. With money, you can put food on the table, keep a roof over your head, or do whatever else you need or desire to do in your life. With money, you can help the poor. You can use money to invest in and build your assets, such as real estate, precious metals, or your knowledge base. You can use money to pay for experiences for yourself and others since, in the end, experiences make up our life.

When you lose the belief that money is optional, you change your outcome because you take very different actions.

2. Relationship Beliefs

If you hold limiting beliefs about the opposite sex—or love relationships in general—you'll either avoid relationships or make promises to your partner that you won't keep. Such a relationship is guaranteed to fail.

Another workshop participant, I'll call her Tina, told me true love was what she wanted more than anything. The most absurd statement then fell from her mouth. "There are no normal single men my age out there." Now, I'd estimate that Tina was around thirty-five years old. She was sitting in a room of approximately

500 people, many of whom were in her age bracket. Tina genuinely believed this statement to be true.

I asked the audience, "All single men in your thirties here, please raise your hand." Multiple hands went up, including two men right beside her. Yet Tina seemed unconvinced. I asked her to consider how many billions of people live on the planet, then asked how she, or anyone, could claim that there were no decent single men their age available. The world today has an abundance of everything—as never before, in fact.

Yet there are any number of common limiting beliefs that rule this arena.

"I'm unworthy of love," an unconscious belief that is often due to low self-esteem or past experiences of rejection or abandonment, is a prime example. If you have this belief, you're likely to sabotage relationships or settle for less than you deserve.

"Love is conditional." Maybe you believe that love must be earned through meeting certain expectations or criteria, which will lead to feelings of insecurity and anxiety in relationships. You'll constantly seek validation and approval from your partners.

"I'll never find true love" is a pessimistic outlook often stemming from past heartbreaks or failed relationships. Believe this and you'll feel resigned to a life of loneliness or believe that finding lasting love is impossible for you.

"I'm better off alone." While independence is healthy, this belief can lead to isolation and a reluctance to open to the possibility of love and intimacy. We can agree that this is not good.

"All relationships end in heartbreak" is a belief that springs from a fear of intimacy and vulnerability. This stems from past experiences of betrayal or emotional pain. Believe this and you'll avoid commitment or sabotage relationships to protect yourself from potential heartache.

"I always attract the wrong partners." This belief involves a pattern of attracting partners who are emotionally unavailable, toxic, or incompatible. Believe this and you're likely to repeat unhealthy relationship patterns without recognizing your role in perpetuating them.

Overcoming these limiting beliefs requires self-awareness, introspection, and a willingness to challenge and reframe negative thought patterns.

3. Self-Agency Beliefs

Most of us will be wronged at one time or another. But it only holds us back if we allow it. Drop the victim mindset for your own sake.

Yet another of my workshop participants told me that her husband never let her do things that made her happy, and she couldn't go anywhere or express herself openly. Nina hadn't gone further than two minutes into her story before I spotted her primary limiting belief system—her penchant to see herself as a victim.

Because I saw the world through the same lenses for such a long time, I knew her life would not change until she began to value herself and to take responsibility for her own life. (By the way, today she's free because she stopped playing the victim, took matters into her own hands, and stepped out of the relationship that confined her. Today she does things that bring her joy.)

I heard all the signs of her victim mentality: blaming others or external factors for her problems, setbacks, and failures (rather than taking responsibility for her actions or choices); a sense of powerlessness in the face of challenges or adversity; a passive attitude (which looks like waiting for others to rescue or solve problems).

She clearly had a negative outlook on life, saw the world as unfair, hostile, or unjust. She seemed to focus on the negative aspects of her situation, dwell on past grievances, and expect the worst outcomes, which only perpetuated the cycle of pessimism and resignation. Then there was the self-pity, her resistance to change, her tendency to view herself as a martyr, her desire for sympathy. I could go on and on.

It's no wonder people with a victim mindset often experience recurring patterns of victimization in their lives, such as repeatedly finding themselves in abusive relationships, financial hardship, or professional setbacks. They unconsciously attract or perpetuate situations that reinforce their sense of victimhood.

Plain and simple, blaming others for outcomes will hold you back. "Whose fault is it?" It's a bad question to ask. Bad questions give you bad answers. A better question might be, *What can I do now; what options are available to me? How can I achieve my goal with resources that are available to me?*

You can't achieve a breakthrough in life until you accept responsibility for your own thoughts, feelings, actions, and results. People who succeed don't make excuses, grimace, or complain; instead, they press on even when they're scared. They keep going even when they lack the desire, will, or motivation to do so. They tell themselves, "I'll do it because I committed to it. I'll do it because I promised, because I want to raise up my life and the lives of others to a higher level."

If you want to achieve what you were put on the earth to do, stop playing the victim. It doesn't serve you. Some people assume the role of a victim by blaming others, making excuses, or continuously recounting a story that hinders their growth. This behavior is often noticeable through their words and actions. Others may adopt a more covert victim mentality, presenting excuses or narratives that seem entirely justified. Both believe someone or something else is responsible for their misfortune or for them not yet achieving their results. You cannot control what other people do, you can only control how you react to what they do.

However, true progress begins with taking full responsibility for your situation and results. You remain a victim until you choose to move forward, forgive, and accept accountability. To transform from a victim to a victor, stop repeating the story that doesn't serve you. Instead, start telling a new story—the story you want to live.

Are you still unsure if you play the role of a victim? If you haven't achieved your goal yet, you most probably do.

Take a Critical Look

Just as a gardener must first clear away the weeds and prepare the soil before planting new seeds, you must address and change old habits and patterns before you can achieve a breakthrough in life. Without this preparation, new growth cannot thrive.

You've taken the initial inventory. Now you need to do some weeding, as it were. Take some time for self-awareness, introspection, and a willingness to examine your thoughts, emotions, and behaviors critically. Here are the basic dance steps you can take to continue to identify your limiting beliefs:

Step 1: Notice negative thought patterns.

Pay attention to recurring negative thoughts or self-talk that undermine your confidence, self-esteem, or sense of worth. These may include thoughts such as "I'm not good enough," "I'll never succeed," or "I'm destined to fail." Stop thinking or saying words out loud that don't serve you, or you don't want to become your reality.

Step 2: Reflect on past experiences.

Consider past experiences, particularly those involving challenges, setbacks, or failures; examine how you interpreted and internalized those experiences. Notice if certain beliefs or assumptions emerged from those experiences, shaping your perceptions and behaviors. Is there something that was OK to believe in the past, but now you can let go? Regardless of how your past experiences have shaped you, don't waste time and energy analyzing your past over and over again. Any belief that no longer serves you can be changed because you are not a victim, but a victor!

Step 3: Identify areas of resistance.

Notice areas of your life where you feel stuck, unmotivated, or resistant to change. Explore what underlying beliefs or fears may be contributing to your resistance and holding you back from taking action or pursuing your goals. Find a question that will help you get unstuck, such as, *How can I create, achieve, change, or overcome?*

Step 4: Notice emotional triggers.

Pay attention to situations or events that trigger strong emotional reactions, such as fear, anger, or self-doubt. These emotional responses can provide clues about underlying beliefs or insecurities that may be influencing your reaction. Replace unwanted reactions with new desired ones.

Step 5: Challenge assumptions.

Question the validity and truthfulness of your beliefs by examining evidence that supports or contradicts them. Consider alternative perspectives, interpretations, or possibilities that may challenge your existing beliefs and broaden your understanding.

Step 6: Find people who achieve what you want to achieve.

Look for people who achieved the goals you want to achieve regardless of their circumstances. Observe what they have done in spite of the limitations they had so that you can do the same.

Step 7: Seek feedback from others.

Ask trusted friends, family members, or mentors for their perspective on your beliefs and behaviors. They may offer insights or observations that you hadn't considered, helping you gain a more objective view of your limiting beliefs. Beware: anytime you're looking for feedback, ask yourself if these people are competent to comment on / judge your beliefs because they may not have the same experiences, knowledge, and goals as you.

Step 8: Journal and reflect.

Journaling can be a helpful tool for exploring your thoughts, emotions, and beliefs in more depth. Write freely about your experiences, feelings, and perceptions, and look for patterns or recurring themes that may indicate underlying limiting beliefs. Write also about what you want to create and achieve in your everyday life.

Step 9: Explore coaching.

Consider seeking support from a coach or joining groups that can help you explore and challenge your limiting beliefs in a supportive and non-judgmental environment—someone who can provide guidance, strategy, and perspective to help you overcome barriers and achieve personal growth.

By engaging in these practices consistently and with an open mind, you can gradually uncover and identify your limiting beliefs, allowing you to challenge and replace them with more empowering and supportive beliefs that align with your goals and aspirations.

EXERCISE: Clean Up Your Limiting Beliefs

1. Write down all your beliefs about the selected area of your life that limits you.

2. Which beliefs aren't working for you and are taking you away from your objectives?

3. Write down all the current beliefs you have that are assisting you on your way to a breakthrough.

4. Write down any new beliefs that you could / should adopt to help you achieve a breakthrough.

Replace Limiting Beliefs with New Beliefs

If the stories you are currently telling yourself are ugly, stop repeating them; they don't serve you. Stop pitying yourself and blaming others. Instead, accept responsibility for your actions and your life. Begin to tell yourself a new story, aloud or in your head. And do this *now*:

I Believe that I'm capable.

I Believe that I'm worthy.

I Believe that I deserve this breakthrough.

I Believe that it is possible.

I Believe that it is possible, even if I don't know what the journey will be like.

> I Believe that I'll find a way, even if I don't know where to start at the moment.

Awaken the victor within you. Allow this giant, who dares to dream big and knows you're deserving and capable of so much more, to awaken and come forth. Allow this giant within you to take the first step out of your comfort zone alongside you. Summon all the resources and potential within you.

I know what you're thinking. *Easy for him to say!* But once you have removed the obstacles and limiting beliefs, you'll be able to see your potential and believe in yourself far more easily. You have immense potential within you. I see what self-belief does for a person nearly every single day.

Ava, for instance, was broke. Her husband had left her without a penny to her name. After a long, protracted divorce, she went to the library and flipped through one of my books. There she found a free audio recording, which led her to one of my workshops. To say she was scared when she arrived is an understatement. She was in a bad state, with no idea what to do next. Her limiting beliefs were evident in nearly every statement she made, in every story that she told: low self-worth, undeserving of love, undeserving of a new beginning, no faith in herself or the world at large. To her, life was a dead end.

We put her in a better state and anchored it in. Then we set clear goals. We imagined her new life on a timeline, zoomed off into the future, so that she could feel it in the present moment. She ran it through her mind until she experienced it—until she knew where she was headed, until she knew what it looked and felt like. That's what got her beyond the self-doubt. She could imagine a very different existence and feel she deserved it. When she left the three-day event, she was a completely different person. She was in a much better state. Her darkness was replaced with smiles, hope, and joy. Absolute freedom. And today she lives a new life.

Crowd Out the Nasty Stories

There are several things you can do to crowd out those nasty stories you tell yourself in favor of your limiting beliefs; here are a few examples . . .

1. Fill your mind with new patterns and concepts.

Use autosuggestion to program and feed your mind with positive ideas, phrases, and sentences. This might include mantras and affirmations. Listen to hypnotic audio recordings or use messaging techniques to bypass the conscious mind and communicate directly with the unconscious. Or record yourself speaking your new beliefs, the ones you listed in the previous exercise, and listen to them while you drive, or even while you sleep. This will help you to regularly reinforce empowering beliefs and attitudes.

2. Make use of hypnosis and self-hypnosis.

The fact is, we're under hypnosis twenty-four hours a day, seven days a week. We simply aren't aware of it most of the time. So, why not get some pointed guidance? Learn how to use hypnotic language patterns on yourself or help others. (By the way, your parents were the first to hypnotize you, even though they weren't expert hypnotists). Perhaps, some of this you will need to undo. You are the most powerful hypnotist for yourself as every hypnosis is self-hypnosis. You're the one with the most power over yourself. Pump yourself up. You'll find a training video and additional resources that will help you to do this at http://aleksandersinigoj.com/victor.

3. Practice mindfulness and meditation.

The goal is to cultivate awareness of your thoughts, emotions, and beliefs so you can identify and challenge limiting beliefs and replace them with more empowering ones. You can also use visualization techniques during your meditation to mentally rehearse your desired outcomes and experiences. (This is self-hypnosis, too.)

4. Reframe negative thoughts and beliefs.

Turn them upside down, into more optimistic and empowering perspectives, and consciously choose to focus on solutions rather than problems.

5. Surround yourself with symbols and imagery.

Create a vision board filled with pictures that represent your goals and aspirations. Hang this board where you will see it several times a day, like in your office or even in your bathroom. (I will explain more in the following chapters.)

6. Surround yourself with positive people.

Positive people think, talk, and act differently than negative people. Their influence is invaluable. They can help you drown out the voices of all those who don't believe in you and the energy vampires that drain your energy.

7. Seek good role models.

Observe them, ask them questions, and incorporate their good practices into your model of the world and into your own life. If you see a happy couple who have been in love for decades, ask them the secret of their success. If you meet a successful athlete, inquire about her model of thinking. And if you come across a successful entrepreneur or leader, ask him for his formula for success. Model excellence in all aspects of life. Try to get to the core of their belief system, what makes it (and them) unique and successful. Then adopt these beliefs as your own.

8. Act as if.

Imagine you're already someone who has achieved a breakthrough. Think, speak, and act as if you've already accomplished the desired objective, as if you've already changed. Before writing my first book I remember playing a game called "Act as if you're already successful." I was signing blank pieces of paper and pretending to hand them out to people as if they were my books that I just signed. It felt stupid at that time, but I tried it. Remember, fake it until you make it. Anyhow, some years later I remember my hand hurting from having signed so many books after one of my workshops. It works; you just need to do it.

9. Reverse engineer your belief system.

In the business world, this is a well-known concept, utilized by innovators like Steve Jobs. Reverse engineering is a technique that works backwards from the end product to the initial step needed to make it. If you want to complete a marathon in three months, what would you need the day of the race; the night before; the week of the race; the month before the race; two months before the race—how would you train; how would you see yourself; how would you see the world? Adopt it.

Once you're on the path, know that there will be occasions when you will have to confront new and different limiting beliefs. However, they will be significantly less limiting than those from the past. And you will be able to detect and eliminate such beliefs much faster, with practice.

Begin with what you know isn't serving you and find ways to change your internal world to attract what you want in life—to achieve a breakthrough. Learn how to influence your unconscious mind; learn how to create long-lasting changes by accessing and reprogramming your deep-seated beliefs, thoughts, and behaviors. You'll find a free hypnotic workshop at https://aleksandersinigoj.com/victor.

The key: take responsibility for yourself and your life—both the inner and external aspects; then, liberate yourself from all the limitations that others have imposed on you, consciously or unconsciously, or that you have allowed them to impose on you. Once liberated, you can act. You are free to design your life the way you want it as long as you do not harm other people. Now it's time to paint the exact picture of what it is you're after, the vision, so you can work towards it.

Remember to approach the process with patience, persistence, and an open mind, as changes in the unconscious may take time to manifest fully.

Envisioning all that you stand to gain in minute detail is purely and simply a mental construct, a game.

5

ENVISION YOUR OUTCOME

It's not what you look at that matters, it's what you see.
—Henry David Thoreau

D uring a vacation in Greece, my family and I spent a day at a particularly wellknown, UNESCOprotected beach. After hours of enjoying this beautiful spot, we returned to town, absolutely starving. We stopped at a local restaurant since the kids wouldn't stop bugging us about when, where, and what we were going to eat! I hadn't noticed it right away, so intent on getting my family fed and quiet, but all the other restaurants were empty. They looked like haunted houses because not a single, living soul seemed to occupy any of the tables. The restaurant we'd chosen, on the other hand, was packed with customers.

We were greeted by a kind and polite man, two qualities I very much value. While we waited for a table, I observed the hustle and bustle and attempted to figure out the tactics behind their success.

When a table for six became ready, another nice waiter brought us to our seats. The service was exceptional; we felt like we were the only customers in the restaurant and that all the staff were dedicated solely to us. I asked every waiter who came to our table what they thought set them apart from the other restaurants, which were standing empty. Every last one of them praised their neighbors and stated that they, too, provided delicious cuisine. In fact, they didn't utter a single word against them.

Later, I got the opportunity to meet the owner, who kept busy in the kitchen, but greeted customers whenever he could. We even took a group photo as a keepsake. The owner was a friendly man, with a great sense of humor. In an instant, he'd even made our youngest giggle, who was by that time exhausted and (how shall I say) in a subpar mood.

I asked the owner for his recipe for success. He explained it to me in two words: customer experience. From the start, he had a vision to give his customers the best possible experience. He had succeeded, I acknowledged. The experience was engaging from the minute you entered the restaurant until the minute you walked out, so he'd lived up to all that he'd imagined.

Much like that restaurant owner, your vision must come first. Every subsequent action you take will serve to bring that vision to reality. Without it, you'll meander about, with no clear direction, and little success.

Give Your Unconscious Mind a Destination

Where do you want to go? Envision it, in minute detail. This is purely a mental construct, a game. The more you hold this sharp image in your thoughts, the more you'll grow accustomed to it, and it will feel natural to you. Pursuing it will feel like the obvious choice to make.

Without this clear destination, your unconscious mind will take you someplace you may not want to go. No map can help. How will you even know when you arrive? You may come to a junction and wonder which way to go, but it makes no difference because you have no idea where you want to go.

Sure, you're aware that turning left will lead you to a completely different destination than turning right, but what difference will it make, really? If your objective is the journey itself, then OK because you have a goal of sorts; otherwise, you'll be aimlessly wasting your energy and an unrenewable resource—time. Why would anyone choose to do that?

Your unconscious mind is your helpmate in getting where you want to go. Think of it as your personal GPS. Everything you program into your unconscious mind is remembered by it. What you might chalk up to coincidence is actually a clear vision stored there.

Long ago, I envisioned visiting the Great Wall of China. I could see it all so clearly, right down to the bricks in the wall and the stars in the sky. Years later, I was invited to give a lecture in China, not just once, but twice. Sure enough, after one lecture, we had dinner just beneath the section of the Great Wall of China that I had in my vision—in my projection. All the details clicked right into place.

Your big, clear breakthrough vision is what will keep you going and moving forward in the right direction. Your vision is the compass that will always direct you towards your goal. When that vision is connected to your "why," it will be that much easier to get out of bed in the morning and make a difference in your life because the vision itself will pull you forward.

It's vital to see yourself as successful in the area where you'd like to experience your breakthrough. It's critical that you see yourself finding or altering something; investing your energy and doing something; receiving the money, job, relationship, and health that you desire in exchange for this action.

Once you know where you're going, you can start pinpointing the details of your journey so your unconscious mind can transmit a clear roadmap.

Your Vision May Be Incomplete

I will freely admit there are obstacles in the way of creating a crystal-clear vision, particularly if you have little experience doing so, for whatever reason. So, before we jump into creating a powerful vision, let's address some common obstacles.

To start, when your vision becomes reality, you will live a very different life than you do now. You need to be fully prepared for that, which is why we set the stage in previous chapters—values, beliefs, anchors, strategies, identity, and so on; they must be evaluated and adjusted if you want to behave differently. In fact, they must be constantly evaluated and adjusted.

A common problem—and one you may face—when creating a vision, is having an idealized version of what you're after playing in your head. You don't see all that it entails, just one distorted segment of it. This sets you up for frustration and disappointment.

It's something akin to romantic movies on the big screen. Watch too many and you might forget the story unfolding before your eyes is a dramatization and far removed from the reality of love. In a movie, a happy relationship is one in which everything blossoms: the couple doesn't have to agree on who will do the pickup from school or the nursery, who will wash the dishes, who will tidy up, or who will change the diapers. What you see in a movie is a few joyful moments, with the implication that the couple will live happily ever after. In real life, we know a relationship requires love, patience, persistence, understanding, respect, trust, and many other qualities.

You may also find that you have an incomplete vision, which can cause dissatisfaction.

I'd been traveling all over the world and lecturing in several countries, visiting places I'd always wanted to see. And yet I wasn't feeling entirely satisfied. Because my family stayed at home, I was almost always alone. I recognized that I'd been vague when it came to setting goals and developing my breakthrough vision board. The pictures and visuals that I'd been using in my breakthrough vision board for my career did not include my family. When I realized this, I instantly incorporated them into my breakthrough vision board. Shortly afterwards, I was invited to give a speech in Japan, and my entire family of six came along with me. As a rule, I now only accept lecture requests from other countries if I can bring my family with me. And for me, this is the most beautiful thing. You too need to design your life the way you want it.

Then there's the simple fact that you may be terrified of your vision.

Make Your Vision Really Big

I'm going to say something that might make you nervous. Your vision must be big. It must be so big that achieving even a fraction of it will give you a sense of accomplishment; if your vision is too small, you won't notice when you achieve it. You'll feel as though you haven't accomplished much in life. If you're not at least a bit afraid of your vision, if it's not at least a little inaccessible to you, it's not big enough. As Norman Vincent Peale once said, "Shoot for the moon. Even if you miss, you'll land among the stars." And shooting for the moon can feel scary.

Personally, my vision from the start has been to be "the best," first in my own country, then in the whole world. After reading a post by Robin Sharma, I remember thinking, *why would you want to be the best in the world, when you can be the best of all time?* I recently expanded my vision: to be the best trainer and coach of all time.

Maybe you think I'm exaggerating, but the bigger the vision, the more likely you are to go far beyond what you'd have imagined possible. A big vision will also provide you with greater drive and a stronger desire to continue learning and growing and pushing the boundaries.

The problem with big dreams is that they may inspire criticism, which may cause you to doubt yourself. So be cautious with whom you share your dreams.

It has been a long road from where I started to where I am now. But today, I'm publishing books, lecturing, and helping people all over the world. I'm following my purpose with heart and energy. My work provides a living for my family and my team. But in between then and now, there were many ups and downs. People mocked me at first. They wrote evaluations and reviews criticizing me as a speaker and advised me to pursue another career. They said that no one needed what I was offering or would pay for my services, that it was all a waste of time. But none of this stopped me. My vision was greater and stronger than all the negative comments. I knew that every comment I received, unfavorable or not, was a reflection of the person who made it.

Such people are simply not ready to accept responsibility for their own lives. I hope that someday they do and that together we can make this world a better place, but that is neither here nor there.

A bonus of dreaming big: you can inspire those around you. Maybe you can't even imagine how good an example you can be for someone who has a dream but doesn't dare to go further. What if you were his or her lighthouse?

If you want your children to be successful and happy in life, allow them to dream and encourage them to achieve their goals (just keep in mind that their goals and desires aren't the same as yours). You can inspire them to do so, by doing the same.

Your vision too should be greater than the negative remarks that may come your way. They should motivate you to preserve and pursue your purpose or mission. Know that it's worthwhile.

Clarity of Vision is Key

A vision is much more than a picture; it's a mental movie filled with visuals, sounds, feelings, scents, and even tastes. This is a *real* vision. Athletes use these mental movies all the time throughout their training. These moment-to-moment movies are often the difference between winning and losing for them. They can see the starting line, the competitors poised for takeoff. They can hear the starting gun go off, the sound of their first footsteps. They can smell their sweat, the dust kicked up by their feet. They can feel their muscles kick into high gear, their steady breath. They can envision every second, right up to the time they cross the finish line and claim their trophy.

Those who outperform the norm and succeed in their field, athletes and restaurant owners included, have a clear vision of where they want to go, plain and simple. They continuously think about what they want; they have a great vision in their heads that they believe in and see opportunities where others see hurdles. They also communicate their vision in a variety of ways to those who may be able to assist them or are a part of this vision. For maximum success, you too will want to include in your vision all the people and areas of your life that are significant to you.

Just for a moment, imagine you're hiring someone to create a movie about your vision. What instructions would you give them so that they could shoot this movie with all the actors involved? What kind of script would you write? Consider all the details and write them down so that you and this filmmaker can both understand them.

Being clear about your vision means you can articulate it in a measurable way; that if someone were to listen to you as you discuss it, they'd be able to sketch it. The more certain you are about your vision, the more likely it is that you'll attain it. Be as specific as possible when describing your end objective, your specific goals, and desires.

I recommend that your vision include health, vitality, and positivity because it will be difficult to accomplish breakthroughs in your life and profession if you aren't in good health.

This vision should involve the people you care about, too, so that you might share pleasant, beautiful, and wonderful moments with them.

Remember to include yourself, as well. It's critical that you picture yourself not only successful, financially free, healthy, loving, loved, serene, joyous, appreciative, positive, fun, and so on, but also happy.

An important aspect of a complete and comprehensive vision should be that you're happy and love the life that you have envisioned and established for yourself. It should be planned in a way that suits you.

By keeping this ideal movie in your mind at all times, you trick your mind into embracing your vision as your new reality. Tell yourself what you want to achieve over and over again, and when you come across a roadblock or difficulty, tell yourself that you're stronger than any obstacle that stands between you and your vision. As a result, your mind will begin to steer your activities in accordance with your vision.

Not Everybody Is Worthy of Your Confidence

Now, once your vision is set, be cautious with whom you share your aspirations.

Speaking about your vision with those you trust can be extremely beneficial. There's something about saying it out loud—about making your intentions known—that allows you to realize it's attainable and to begin believing in it.

It may be difficult to discuss your dreams and vision with those who don't believe in them, who mock you or otherwise put you down. It's important to remember that those who doubt your vision or even laugh at you are acting on their own limiting beliefs. Perhaps it's because they don't believe in themselves and feel incapable of achieving such a vision. Or perhaps they're afraid that if you realize your great vision, they'll lose you.

You don't have to share your vision with anyone if you feel those around you will add to your limiting beliefs, or if you feel particularly shy doing so. However, in such moments, it's important that your vision is truly grand and that you have internalized it—that you feel it and can repeat it.

You May Also Lose People Along the Way

When you internalize your new vision, you'll begin to transform. When you begin to transform and become different from the person you were before, you may encounter friction. You'll have to accept that you have changed and help those around you do the same.

However, despite your best efforts, some people will be unable to accept your change and may even walk out of your life. In time, you'll be able to look back and realize there was a reason why they left; therefore, don't be sad about it. Maybe they were in your life for a certain period of time to teach you a particular life lesson, and now their work is done. Maybe they were an obstacle on your path to success; maybe you blocked their path as well, so they couldn't change.

New people will appear who understand your big dreams and your breakthrough vision, and they'll accompany you on your journey. Some will be with you for a short time, others will remain with you for the rest of your life. But you don't have to try to be like them; you don't have to resemble them. Be unique. Because you *are* unique. Walk your path, trust in your path, and have your great breakthrough vision in mind at all times.

Your Vision Will Morph

When you grow, so does your vision. This means your vision will change over time. Don't let it scare you.

Warren Buffett, co-founder, chairman, and CEO of Berkshire Hathaway, is an innovator by nature. A serial entrepreneur even while in high school, he's known for seeing beyond what others think is possible. Skeptical of active management and the pack mentality of investors, he believed he could outperform the market in the long run and advised both individual and institutional investors to move their money to low-cost index funds that track broad, diversified stock market indexes. He claimed that, when trillions of dollars are managed by Wall Streeters charging high fees, it would usually be the managers who reaped outsized profits, not the clients. And his vision made him one of the most successful business owners of all time.

If you don't change and continually modify your vision, if your vision does not expand, you'll remain where you are now. Today, the world is developing and learning quicker than ever before, and it appears that we're being overtaken on both sides. Your breakthrough vision will make you expansive and more alive, and it will continually propel you towards your objectives and desired results.

Remember that your vision will not only help you to achieve what you want, get what you desire, even assist others in ways you desire—it will help you become the person you want to be.

The danger of having such a vision is that it always pulls you onward. You'll be constantly challenging the status quo. Once you've imbibed your grand vision, once your unconscious mind has embraced it, it's over—it's over with lazing about in your comfort zone. You'll constantly be propelled forward towards it.

EXERCISE: Paint a Clear Breakthrough Vision

It's time to build a vision that will inspire you, a vision that you'll be proud of, and most importantly, a vision that will pull you along and make your breakthrough a reality.

Think of the area you chose at the beginning of this book and where you want to make a breakthrough.

1. Write down your big dreams, your clear breakthrough vision (your goal).

2. Allow yourself to dream without any obstacles or constraints.

3. Be as precise as possible and use the present tense.

4. Describe what you see, hear, smell, taste, or feel on reaching your vision.

5. Who is with you in your vision?

6. Describe your day in six months/one year/three years in accordance with your vision.

7. Where do you see yourself in one year, five years, ten years?

A good and positive aspect of having a vision is that you can begin constructing it at any point in your life. Because you *are* starting over. Because a new day is dawning. Because it's a new moment. You can start all over again, right away. It doesn't matter what you've experienced in life. Your education doesn't matter. It doesn't matter what you've done or not done. It doesn't matter where you live, what (or who) you know.

It only matters that you start with a mental construct, with an idea that you nourish every day until your mind accepts it and it becomes your breakthrough vision.

You might nourish it using selfhypnosis, autosuggestion, or affirmations. You might nourish it by hanging out with like-minded people; by taking small steps towards the desired outcome; by hiring a coach or mentor. You might nourish it using a myriad of methods.

When I first saw the movie *The Secret*, I started making vision boards, repeating affirmations, and listening to hypnosis audios. I purchased a zero gravity chair in the hopes of getting my future vision into my unconscious mind faster and deeper. I put on special glasses to create a deeper trance and used a projector to view it. Using self-hypnosis techniques, I was able to implant my vision into my unconscious mind. To further buttress my vision, I created passwords that served to constantly remind me of what I was after. Iweigh86kgs# is an example.

At times, I was rather afraid of the details I put into the projection—images and visuals that seemed impossible for me at that time. Perhaps you'll experience the same.

But when you have a clear vision of where you want to go and program that vision into your mind you will encounter countless miracles every day that previously seemed unfathomable. And you go about it by programming your mind.

Day in and day out: spend a few seconds imagining your great vision, in vivid detail; when you get up in the morning, envision your perfect day—clearly see what you want to do and achieve, all in accordance with your great vision; before you go to bed, "image" the next day—take a mental snapshot of what it will look like. The more regularly you practice this, the greater the results you'll notice in your life.

EXERCISE: Create a Vision Board

1. Make a vision board and hang it somewhere visible where you can see it every single day, many times a day (if possible).

2. Your vision board should include pictures that represent your future, as well as your breakthroughs in various areas of life.

3. Every day, for half a minute or so, look at your vision board in a healthy emotional state—visualize yourself as successful and see how the images on your board come to life, with you as the main actor.

Version 2.

You can also make a digital vision board. In this way, your vision board will always be with you and accessible throughout your day.

Collect images, short films, and music that motivate you and create a collage or projection.

Victors plan how they'll
get to the outcome
they wish to achieve.

6

DEVELOP A PLAN

———————

You cannot hope to make progress in areas where you have taken no action.

–Epictetus

I n Slovenia, land of snowcapped mountains, emerald-green lakes, intricate cave systems, and winding rivers, we natives know that if you want to go from Koper to Maribor, you must first follow the signs for the capital city of Ljubljana. In fact, we plan on this slight detour. Koper, in case you're curious, is considered one of the oldest towns in the country. It was originally built during the Middle Bronze Age on what was then a rocky island very near the shore inhabited by goats. Maribor, another city most definitely worth visiting, has a medieval center, cobblestone streets at every turn, a rich history linked with the nearby wine-growing region, and beautiful surroundings. Yet you cannot get from one worthwhile destination to the other without passing through Ljubljana, the only place where helpful signs seem to exist. There you'll see a sign pointing toward Maribor, another one toward Koper. Without these signs, an innocent tourist would be completely out of luck. They'd have no idea which direction to head because no other signs exist. Tourists don't know enough to plan for a pitstop in Ljubljana.

Having the right plan to get you where you want to go, that desired place you've envisioned, is essential. You will not get there otherwise, at least not easily. You know what area of life you'd like to improve, at least as a start. You've locked in on a dream. You see the bright shiny goal you're after. You have a vision for it. But now we've got to do something about it. And that requires coming up with a plan.

Your vision must answer the question of where you're going, and your plan must tell you how you'll get there. You must plan your success, the result, and the desired breakthrough.

If you desire a million dollars, make a plan to obtain it. What kind of business will you start and when? What will you sell? How much income will you need to bring in each month? This may sound decidedly unromantic, but if you want a romantic relationship, make a plan. Decide to go out on three dates a week until you find the person of your dreams. Or tell everyone you know what kind of person you're looking for and ask for introductions. If you want to lose weight, be healthier, and have more energy, you need a plan, one that no doubt includes more activity and a healthy diet, as well as, perhaps, reaching out to an expert in this field. If you want to achieve a company growth breakthrough, your plan will likely contain actions and examples of how you can help and serve others, how you can develop and generate meaningful value, and how you can share this with as many people as possible.

Without a plan, you will do things haphazardly. You'll drive around Slovenia with no idea where you're headed. Your plan is a bridge between where you are (Maribor) and where you want to be (Koper).

Plans are Born of Vision

Victors plan how they'll get to the outcome they wish to achieve. Planning shouldn't be viewed as an end in itself, but it should be comprised of practical steps to achieve the intended outcomes. I say this because some people only plan; their problem is that they never go past this stage. Planning is a procedure that may be continually implemented, upgraded, and amended while taking action. If you hit a dead end with your plan, do what a GPS would do—identify a new course and upgrade your plan.

I've observed that the time spent thinking about and preparing to reach goals doesn't simply provide greater clarity and drive, it also produces speedier breakthroughs, both minor and major. The same applies to you: take the time to lay out the steps required to achieve your desired goal. Take the time to think—without your phone, the internet, or any other distraction—and plot your road to success.

Imagine yourself as having made it. Imagine the result you wish to achieve. When you visualize yourself achieving it, go back in your mind and see what steps you took to get there.

Imagine what you need to do, how you need to act to achieve that goal. Ask yourself what the first logical step is—the one you need to take right now to move towards attaining that result. This is where your plan begins.

Maybe you'd like to win an Olympic medal—that's the big goal. Your plan might be quite simple: a broad variety of workouts and exercises with the necessary expert support, a sound nutritional regimen, which you will follow daily until the day of the competition. The details of a successful plan to win an Olympic medal are likely more involved than this, but these steps would go a long way towards achieving that end. Further steps would be included over time because of the growing awareness of what is required.

A Rough Plan Is Better Than No Plan

People frequently fail to establish any kind of a plan because their vision isn't totally clear, and they aren't perceiving all the essential steps to attain it. It doesn't matter if your goal is to win an Olympic gold or to advance in your profession, if you don't know what steps are needed to get you there, you may become fearful and begin convincing yourself that you don't have the knowledge to accomplish it or doubt whether you're even capable of achieving it.

This is what happened to me.

When I first encountered my mentors and saw them speaking on stage, I wondered, *when will I ever give such a speech; when will*

I have these special light effects; when will I have all of this? But then I thought to myself, *step by step, Aleksander. Make a plan to achieve this. Take the first step, the second step, the third step. Don't compare yourself to your mentors, but only to yourself—where you were before versus where you are now.*

Now I'm walking—just like they are—towards my goal, improving my plan. Constantly.

Your initial plan may not be perfect, but it need not be. An imperfect plan is better than no plan at all. You just need to know the first few steps needed to move closer to realizing your vision. Use all your current knowledge. You don't have to work out every step right away. Sometimes knowing the key steps and/or the one or two steps ahead of you will get you headed in the right direction.

With each new facet of knowledge and experience, you'll get better and will be able to improve your plan correspondingly. You can revise, rewrite, update, and improve your plan until you achieve it. Take your next step in a positive mental state towards your desired goal and trust that when you do this, you will get new learnings and insights to continue.

Draw It Out on Paper

You can make your plan visual by drawing it, or you can create a list of ten bullet points. Your plan can be made on a napkin left over from your lunch. Your plan, as I've said, need not be perfect, but it should include all the steps you currently believe are most accessible and doable at the moment.

I'm continuously writing, drawing, and sketching something; and sometimes the ideas I transfer from my thoughts to paper are absolutely illegible. I have dozens of notebooks filled with notes. I often don't even look back over these notes; in the process of putting down the planned activities on paper, I've become clear about the plan and the steps I need to take to reach my objective. This is how I do all my planning, as it helps me clarify the actions I need to take and my overall plan. The process also enables me to constantly program my mind.

All you'll need is a pen and a piece of paper. Write out the steps that will take you to your goal; write the date you intend to complete each step; and keep your plan in a visible spot so you can see it at all times.

EXERCISE: Create Your First Step-by-Step Plan

1. Identify the first logical step.

2. Write out all the additional steps that you can think of that you must undertake to attain your goal.

3. Make a list of what you intend to do.

4. Make a commitment to yourself that you'll attain your vison, and don't forget to include a time frame.

5. Who will help you?

Other Plan Essentials

Don't forget to include people who could assist you in implementing your plan more quickly and easily and anyone you'd like to accomplish it alongside.

Whatever plan you decide to develop, make sure the ground rules are as plain as day. Then stick to those rules and the plan. Within the rules, the structure, and the plan, you'll find a hidden freedom—the success and the outcome you seek.

Don't forget to include how you intend to track your progress so you know you're on course and that the plan is assisting you in accomplishing the vision you've set for yourself. What you can measure, you can improve. Measure how successfully you're carrying out the specific steps of the plan. If you discover that you aren't getting the expected outcomes, modify your plan or the way you apply it.

What This Looks Like

Let us imagine that you want to create a plan to double your income in the year ahead. To achieve this goal, here's what your step-by-step plan might look like . . .

Step 1: Set clear income goals.

Determine exactly how much money you would need to earn to double your income by December 31. What value can you create or add to do that?

Step 2: Identify income streams.

Explore various income streams or opportunities that can contribute to doubling your income before May 1. This may include increasing sales or revenue in your current job or business, increasing the frequency of how often people buy from you, pursuing freelance work or side gigs, investing in income-generating assets, or exploring new career opportunities.

Step 3: Assess current skills and resources.

Evaluate your current skills, expertise, and resources that can be leveraged to increase your income, and which ones can be most easily and quickly monetized. Identify areas where you can improve or acquire new skills that are in demand in your industry or market. Do this by or before June 6.

Step 4: Network and collaborate.

Connect with mentors, peers, industry experts, and potential collaborators who can provide guidance, support, and opportunities to help you achieve your income goals more quickly and easily. List the names by February 28. Then build relationships and seek out partnerships that can accelerate your progress. Start with the first relationship by March 5.

Step 5: Create milestones.

Break down your income goal into smaller, manageable milestones, and create an action plan outlining specific steps and tasks to achieve each one. List the deadlines and prioritize tasks based on their importance and impact on your income before your vacation in April.

Step 6: Invest in personal development.

Invest in your personal and professional development by attending workshops, training programs, or online courses that can enhance your skills, knowledge, and capabilities. Hire a business coach or consult with someone who has achieved the goal you want to achieve. Continuous learning and growth are essential for increasing your earning potential. Pick the first course by July 1.

Step 7: Maximize current income sources.

Identify opportunities to optimize and maximize your current income sources before the start of Q3. This may involve negotiating a raise or promotion at your current job, increasing prices for your products or services, creating a new funnel, or improving efficiency and productivity to generate more revenue.

Step 8: Diversify income streams.

Explore opportunities to diversify your income streams to reduce risk and increase stability. Consider adding new products or services, expanding into new markets or industries, or investing in passive income streams such as rental properties or dividend-paying stocks. Finish this review by the end of Q3.

Step 9: Track progress and adjust accordingly.

Establish clear metrics and key performance indicators (KPIs) to track your progress towards your income goals. Pick these metrics by March 1. Regularly review, on the first of each month, your progress against these metrics and adjust your strategies and tactics as needed based on insights and feedback.

Step 10: Stay focused and persistent.

Stay focused on your income goals and maintain a positive mindset, even in the face of challenges or setbacks. Be persistent and resilient in pursuing your goals and celebrate your achievements along the way to stay motivated and inspired.

Take the First Step

How do you make your plan a reality? How do you get there? By taking the initial step! Then you take another, and another, and so on. If your goal is to earn one million dollars, make a plan to earn your first dollar. Once you've earned it, devise a strategy for earning the remaining 999,999.

You don't have to be afraid of the road, no matter how long it is. Instead of always worrying about what may go wrong (and not going forward as a result), focus more time and energy on those first steps.

If you're concerned about how you'll complete steps four, five, and six—before you ever begin to take a single step—it's a good sign you've got a plethora of limiting beliefs and fears at play. You may want to go back and revisit those.

And yes, perfectionism is a common limiting belief that shows up during this process. Sometimes the most brilliant and accomplished individuals are their own worst enemies because they think too much and try to be perfect in everything they do. Perfectionism prevents you from ever starting. Perfectionism slows you down, hinders you, and destroys more dreams and goals than fear does. It's never good enough; it's never the right moment; it's never exactly the way it should be for you to begin. You will most definitely want to overwrite this belief.

I'm sure you already know this helpful affirmation or auto-suggestion: "Better done than perfect!" Every time perfectionism gets the better of you, repeat it to yourself. Once, twice, maybe five times. And take the next step.

You'll reach the end of this path sooner or later if you're determined to take the first step, know why you're taking your chosen path, remove obstacles and limiting beliefs, believe in yourself, have a clear vision of where you want to go, and follow the steps you've planned. Step by step, carry out your plan. Watch where your feet are going and mind your step, but keep your gaze fixed on your vision.

Keep those big dreams in mind always, and your reasons for pursuing them—they'll give you the power and inspiration to keep going. You'll learn all you need to know along the way. You don't need the knowledge you'll need later, now—it's impossible to know it now. You do, however, have the knowledge and the capabilities to take that first step. Everything else you'll figure out as you go.

Revise, Revise, Revise

Perhaps you have a lot of learning ahead of you. Great! When you learn something new, revise and improve your plan. Allow mentors, trainers, and coaches—people who have walked this journey before you—to assist you in your planning. Perhaps through learning new information, you'll pick a different course from the one you set out on at the start. No plan is final, and you can update or adjust it when you gain new knowledge or obtain new insights. It's important that you stick to your plan and keep moving towards your goal.

I never stop pondering my plan; I discuss it with my coworkers, mentors, and mastermind group members, and I tweak it. Every time you share your plans with someone, they get clearer; even speaking them aloud to yourself helps. Keep a notepad handy (maybe even more than one), to jot down your vision, what you want to accomplish, and the steps for getting there. Do this repeatedly; it will serve as the basis for a more extensive plan. When you write it out over and over again, it helps acquire clarity.

Remember that planning is like driving your car at night. The headlights of a car only let you see about 350 feet ahead. You can imagine the path and follow it on a map, but you won't actually see the next 350 feet until you move forward 350 feet. If you don't move ahead, you won't be able to see the next leg of your journey. Perhaps you'll face an unexpected obstacle or a "traffic jam," forcing you to take a detour (Ljubljana, anyone?)—however, you'll still know where you're going. You can't improve and polish a plan to perfection so that it can really serve you if you're not using and applying it. Add whatever steps you believe are required to bring your vision and objective to fruition.

Focusing implies directing your attention first and foremost to the activities that yield the greatest value for you.

7

BANISH DISTRACTIONS AND FOCUS

———————

The art of knowing is knowing what to ignore.

–Rumi

You've got a vision; you've got a plan. Your next mission: direct all your energy and focus on moving towards your goals and aspirations. Focus on what you want and ignore what you don't want because anything you focus on gains strength, energy, and the opportunity to flourish.

People who are distracted and do a little bit of everything usually end up not getting the outcomes they want. They're often afraid that if they put all their attention on one thing—if they're focused—they'll miss out on many other opportunities. This is where we get the acronym FOMO (fear of missing out). Unfortunately, this sort of person is unaware that their lack of focus is costing them the chance to make a breakthrough in the one key area in which they really want to succeed. Remember, massive success begins with change in one area, which then triggers further transformation.

As you have probably noticed, top athletes, such as swimmers, don't compete in soccer, basketball, cycling, or tennis at the same time. Instead, they dedicate all their energy to one selected sports discipline. They have a defined objective and are focused on the execution of the training plan that helps them improve in their chosen field. Everything else is subordinated to it. Not only do they ignore other competitive sports, but they also eliminate other "normalized" distractions such as partying and staying up late since they require a lot of energy for the next day's training or competition. They don't hang out with B-level friends in the town square, or take up knitting, or binge-watch TV like a fair percentage of the population.

Like other successful people, these athletes know that focus is something of a magnifying glass . . .

Consider what happens if you move a magnifying glass in sunlight over a sheet of paper. It creates little more than a fleeting shadow over the page. However, if you hold that magnifying glass consistently over the same spot, the paper will begin to burn, or at least change color, depending on how strong the sunlight is and how persistent you are. Similarly, you'll be astonished at what can happen when you concentrate all your energy, strength, determination, and decisiveness in one direction. Focus, focus, focus.

Learn to Say No

When you're determined to create a breakthrough, you must say "no" to everything that isn't taking you towards it.

Warren Buffet has long said that successful people say "no" to almost everything. Nearly every day, Steve Jobs used to ask Apple's former design chief this question: "How many times have you said 'no' today?" He believed saying "no" produces focus. He frequently stated that he was proud of both the things he said "yes" to and the ones he said "no" to. When Jobs returned to Apple, he chose to suspend the production of a number of devices. Now that's focus.

When you say "no" to anything that isn't in line with your vision, you're saying "yes" to your vision.

I know it's not always easy to say "no" to the various "treats" life has to offer. It's not easy to say "no" to hanging out with friends—even those you know aren't your true friends. It's not easy to say "no" to activities and people whom you care about and with whom you enjoy wonderful memories of the past. It's not easy to say "no" to a business opportunity that appears exciting but is unrelated to your purpose. But this is what you need to do when they're not helping you achieve your objective and are only diverting your focus away from your vision and plan.

I repeat, once you've decided to make a breakthrough and have a clear hierarchy of values, a bulletproof breakthrough vision, and a plan for achieving it, you'll find it easier to say "no" to everything that isn't leading you towards your breakthrough, and "yes" to everything that is. It's not easy. But it's simple once you've made up your mind and decided what you want. This is part of success. Your plan will help you maintain focus. It will continually remind you of your objective, the steps you need to take to get there, and the activities to which you'll need to say "no" or "yes."

Pause for just a moment and consider the many things you currently do in your personal and professional life that aren't truly helping you attain your goals and dreams faster. How many activities do you have on your schedule today because you're scared to say "no" to others? What activities are you engaging in while knowing they're robbing you of your time? Could you list them?

If you want to be successful, you must be ruthless and say "no" to all the time-thieves in your life. Be proud of yourself every day when you say "no" to the people and activities that lead you away from success. By focusing on your objective, your vision, and the steps you've planned, you'll see the first results quickly.

Before I go into strategies and tools that will keep you focused as you follow your plan in pursuit of your breakthrough, I'd like to mention a common roadblock along the transformational path: trying to do it all.

When I meet entrepreneurs, I get the impression that they're trying to cover all the bases in their business, and then some. Not only do they take on every single task to look busy (and therefore important), they're constantly looking at ways to pivot to satisfy an interest or to increase their supposed market share. Try a bunch of things at once, they believe, and one will eventually hit success. If they were athletes, they'd be skiing, jumping, swimming, and playing football and basketball all at the same time. They can't figure out why they're not enjoying massive success given the energy they're expending. They continually ask themselves, "Where's my medal? Where's my hard-earned success? Where's my money?"

There is no medal, no success, and no money simply because they're doing too many things outside their circle of expertise. Indeed, they may have numerous talents, several businesses in various sectors, and be a master in different fields, but they have no singular focus or true plan to get them where they most want to be. Most have no clear vision either. They're too busy catching plates they've thrown up in the air.

Multitasking Will Cost You

Entrepreneurs get into the bad habit of not only juggling their interests but also multitasking every minute of the day. Researchers have shown that those who tend to do several things at once, who switch back and forth between different activities, lose a significant number of hours per day because their brains cannot recover from the distraction. Who can focus when you can't even think?

Focusing implies directing your attention first and foremost to the activities that yield the greatest value for you and/or your business. If you want to make a million dollars, for instance, you must concentrate your time on activities that will bring you that million dollars, while delegating or even eliminating all others from your to-do list.

One way an entrepreneur can identify these high-value tasks is to assign an "hourly rate" to every activity they are tempted to handle themselves, as opposed to delegating out. I'll walk you through the calculation.

The mathematical equation for earning one million dollars, a common business goal, is very simple. Let's assume that the average number of working hours per year is 2,000. If you're an entrepreneur, this figure may be a little higher, but for simplicity's sake let's take 2,000 hours. If you divide one million dollars by the number 2,000 you get an hourly rate of 500 dollars. Each activity you engage in must be worth at least 500 dollars per hour, or you "aren't allowed" to do it.

Now, if you happen to be at the beginning of your entrepreneurial path, you'll likely have to step in with all kinds of roles: you're the CEO, personal assistant, salesperson, cleaner, etc. (I know your excuses!) And yes, at the beginning of your journey, you may be required to perform activities with low added value. Whatever the case may be, I want you to constantly ask yourself this simple question: *Is the email I'm sending right now, the time I'm spending surfing the web, or any other of my activities worth 500 dollars per hour, or does it have the potential to be worth 500 dollars or more for my company?* If this isn't the case, it's not for you.

Soon enough, you'll get to a point in your business where you must delegate. When you delegate, you teach your coworkers and team members how to function independently so you can concentrate your time and energy on tasks that provide the greatest added value. For some of us micromanagers, it's hard to let go of the reigns because we feel as though we're the only ones who can do it correctly. And right there is a limiting belief I still have to work on.

Here's a mindset shift that has helped me accomplish numerous breakthroughs and shifts as an entrepreneur but also as a human with big goals: direct your focus on what you're excellent at. For everything else, hire the best people to assist you in accomplishing the things you're not good at. This assistance might be a babysitter, a stockbroker, or a CEO for your company. This is how you open the time and energy to concentrate on just one area. Time and time again, I wasted time and money trying to accomplish things that other people were far better at than me. I tried to do it all; as a consequence, I ultimately lost out. Learn from my mistakes.

Focus On You, Not Others

If you want to create true purpose and meaning in your life, you'll want to make sure your efforts aren't "selfish" but in the service of others. That being said, for now, it's more important to devote all your efforts to your objective and what you want to accomplish than it is to focus on others.

When it comes to pursuing vision, your focus may stray to others in a few different ways.

You may be tempted to encourage others to make a breakthrough of their own, rather than concentrating on yourself and your own goals and plans. You may also be tempted to focus on what others are accomplishing while you're on the path to your own transformation.

Case in point: after being released from the hospital, I decided to take up running. As you would expect, running was far harder than I thought it would be since I was overweight. After a while, I gained stamina and was able to run in earnest. After running for several years, I decided to enter a half marathon at the Ljubljana Marathon, the largest running event held in Slovenia.

On the morning of that marathon, the last Sunday in October, I was surrounded by incredibly good runners. They dictated a tempo that was far faster than mine. Instead of focusing on myself and the rhythm I had practiced and set for myself, I kept glancing at the runners to my left and right, striving to keep up with them. I outpaced myself and flew through the first few miles. If you're a runner, you know what happened. I ran out of energy and barely made it to the finish line. In fact, I was so beat up, I nearly cried when I realized I had to walk a few more blocks to my parked car. I felt like such a wannabe; I flirted with the idea of giving up.

This is what many people do when pursuing their goal: they observe others who may be in better financial, physical, emotional, or whatever shape, and try to copy their exact steps or moves, rather than focusing on the actions appropriate to themselves. Invariably, this leaves them disappointed, demoralized, and convinced that they simply can't compete. If you want a good excuse to give up, this can't be beat.

Learn from others but keep your focus on what you can accomplish right now. Do what is right for you. Keep your eyes on your own well-thought-out plan.

And that means you should not be concerned with what others think—particularly those who haven't achieved what you're seeking. As the Chinese philosopher, Lao Tzu, once said, "Care about what other people think, and you will always be their prisoner." There will always be someone who dislikes what you do or thinks you should do it differently. Those who attack or criticize you are probably unhappy and wounded in themselves; they lack true motivation and a sense of purpose in their own life. If you inadvertently "touch" their wound, even the briefest and most innocuous contact might cause agonizing pain.

The same holds true if you notice your coworkers aren't sufficiently driven, you're having trouble at home or problems communicating with others, your family isn't behind you, and you feel like the whole world is against you. Keep focused on your goal. Don't be distracted by every perceived lack of enthusiasm for your efforts.

EXERCISE: Saying NO

1. How many times did you say "no" today?

2. Make a list of the things you'll say "no" to in the near future, in order to keep focused on making your vision a reality.

Tools and Strategies to Stay Focused

Stay focused. I repeat, stay focused. It's one of the most important aspects of success. When you've identified what gives you (the greatest) added value—be it an action, activity, thought sequence, or what have you—repeat and refine the process, then repeat it again because you've discovered the goose that lays golden eggs. And one way to take good care of that goose is to use tools and strategies that allow you to focus all your attention on it.

1. Affirmations

I often use affirmations to stay focused on my outcome and minimize disruptive thoughts. Here's a list of affirmations you can repeat to keep you working towards your breakthrough:

> I am fully committed to achieving my goal, and I will carry on until I succeed.

> I believe in myself and my abilities to overcome any challenges that come my way.

Every step I take brings me closer to my goal, and I am making progress every day.

I am worthy of success, and I deserve to achieve my goals.

I am motivated, driven, and determined to reach my goals no matter what.

Challenges are opportunities for growth, and I am capable of overcoming them.

I am focused, disciplined, and dedicated to achieving my goals.

I am surrounded by abundance, and success flows effortlessly into my life.

I am resourceful and creative, and I always find solutions to any obstacles in my path.

I attract opportunities and people who support me in achieving my goals.

I am capable of achieving anything I set my mind to, and I am unstoppable.

I trust the process of achieving my goals, and I know that everything is unfolding perfectly.

I am grateful for the progress I've made so far, and I celebrate every small victory along the way.

I am aligned with my purpose, and I am guided by clarity and intuition in pursuing my goals.

I am resilient, persistent, and unstoppable in the pursuit of my dreams.

Choose the affirmations that resonate most with you and repeat them daily, either silently or out loud, to reinforce positive beliefs, boost your confidence, and keep you motivated towards achieving your important goal. Feel free to customize these affirmations to better suit your specific goals and aspirations.

And don't just repeat them, write them down, daily. Then delete everything from your calendar and daily schedule that isn't linked to your goals. Focus on the activities that will provide you with the best outcomes and the greatest added value. To find more affirmations, go to http://aleksandersinigoj.com/victor for the extra training videos and resources that go along with this book.

2. Quiet The Voices

To help you silence all the voices in your head, turn off all distractions, whether internal or external, and commit all your energy and focus to the desired breakthrough in that one area of your life. Switch off any devices that might disrupt your focus.

Trust me, it can be done. This book is a good example; while writing, rewriting, and editing this book, I've not been available by phone or email; I've managed to avoid all other distractions that could steal my time and attention.

Today, too many people and applications compete for your attention. But your breakthrough and success depend entirely on how well you manage your attention and concentration for tasks that truly count.

Disable notifications on your mobile devices and, most importantly, set aside time when your undivided attention is on the task you want to complete successfully. You'll be surprised at how quickly you can make progress if you're focused, bringing your desired breakthrough within reach.

3. Claim the First 90 Minutes

Use the first 90 minutes toward accomplishing your goal. Robin Sharma applies the 90901 rule: for 90 days, devote the first 90 minutes of your working day to the activity that provides you with the most additional value.

This means for three months, every day, for a full hour and a half, you're completely focused on an activity aligned with your plan and vision. Once you reach the last day, you can add another 90 days. You can do just about anything for 90 days.

By being relentlessly focused on your vision you will reach breakthroughs you aren't even aware of yet like nobody's business. From the moment you get up till the moment you go to sleep, you must focus on the outcome and how to ethically attain it—no stepping on toes, no taking advantage of other people, no dismissing your personal and professional responsibilities. Simply do everything within your power to achieve your outcome. Disregard everything else—all the unimportant minutia currently clogging up your mind and day.

When your mind is focused, you'll begin to take consistent action.

EXERCISE: Your Top Three

Focus is sustained one day at a time.

1. Write down the top three results you will achieve today that bring you the most value.

2. Focus on getting it done.

3. Tomorrow repeat steps one and two.

When you go the extra mile,
you'll discover that this route
is never crowded.

8

TAKE CONSISTENT ACTION

Action is the foundational key to all success.

–Pablo Picasso

In his book *Outwitting the Devil*, Napoleon Hill explains why only a handful of people on this planet achieve great success. Read the book, and you'll discover that those who become successful do so because they're determined; they reject limiting beliefs about success, money, or relationships as they progress through life; they have a plan and stay focused; and they are willing to pay the price by sticking with consistent action while in a positive emotional state. They are willing to get out of their comfort zone. They take action, telling themselves: "Yes, I'll do everything that's required," "I'll give my everything to achieve the result I want in life." And they never look for shortcuts.

When an Olympic-level athlete attended my hypnosis workshop, she told the participants that she woke up every day at 5 a.m. and trained in an icy cold swimming pool. She knew consistent and intense practice was required if she was to make the standard for the Olympics and win an Olympic medal. She was disciplined; her training had structure. Most people aren't willing to get up so early in the morning, let alone move their behind, step into a frigid morning, and plunge into a freezing cold pool. They aren't willing to pay the price. Instead, they search for every conceivable work-around or shortcut. They spend more time looking for loopholes than what is required to do the work.

You make the choice. Are you going to be like everyone else, or will you make a breakthrough? Are you going to win your medal, or are you going to stay in your nice, warm bed? Are you willing to pay the price?

Paying the price means there are no shortcuts. Action must be taken. Take action in a positive mental state. Victors always pay the price. It's impossible to achieve a breakthrough simply sitting on the couch while holding the plan for your vision in your hands. A thought can change your perception of reality, but only thoughtful action can change the content of that reality.

Paying the price means that if you want to work out in the gym, you must go there. Period. There is no substitute for activity. There is no substitute for work. If you want to get in shape, there is no substitute for eating nutritious meals and working out regularly. There is no substitute. You may visualize, you may talk about what you want, you may plan for it, but you also need to act in a positive mental state. And you have to do it. I can't do it for you; your trainer can't do it for you. No one else can do it for you.

If you're unwilling to pay the price, if you're unwilling to take action, you won't get your desired results. Even then, you'll pay a price, one way or another (either take action and succeed, or take no action and keep the status quo).

So, I urge you to kick yourself into high gear and tell yourself, "I'm now going to take action; I'm going to move, step by step, towards my goals, towards results." Then proceed. Your actions, not your words, should speak of the happy relationship, healthy body, abundance, or successful career you desire.

The Price You Shouldn't Pay

Make sure the price you're paying for your breakthrough isn't your health or your relationships. Oftentimes, people forget about themselves when chasing their ambitions; they forget what is truly important—their life and physical health. This is what happened to me many years ago, but my heart warned me that if I wanted to reach my goals, I needed to change my lifestyle and mindset. Everything you do must take your health, family, and the people you care about into account.

Take time for yourself; mark out clear boundaries for time with your family or the people dear to you; appreciate yourself and your body. Need motivation? Look at the people who aren't doing this and who are paying a price that will eventually become too great for them to bear—that should give you reason enough. Look at the hierarchy of their values and the conflicts in their internal world—that should help you discover your reasons.

There's a fine line.

The price I had to pay for the knowledge I have today can't be quantified in monetary value. It's not the financial investment I've been required to make; it's how many times I've been away from my family, how many times I've had to travel abroad at times when the company was its busiest, how many sleepless nights, how many weekends I've worked, how many times I've gone straight to work after an overnight flight, with no sleep at all ... Yet still I say to myself, "I'm doing this because I know it's part of my plan to be the best of all time."

But I also know the price of continually investing in myself. Growing and expanding my knowledge cannot overshadow the value I place on my family. This is the tightrope I walk. You may need to do the same. For now, just start slow. Take the first action step and have faith in yourself.

Starting slow could also keep you from taking unethical shortcuts to get ahead faster, which is another price you should never pay. You will want to achieve your goals the proper and fair way, without taking unnecessary risks.

For instance, if you want to achieve a fit and healthy body, using illicit substances or doping might be tempting, but the long-term consequences could leave you worse off than before you began pursuing true excellence. Business growth, if that's what you wish to achieve, should be achieved in compliance with the law and without causing harm to others. Make every effort to be honest and sincere. Make every effort to choose the path that's best for you—one that you can be proud of.

Even if others encourage you to take a shortcut, stand your ground. Shortcuts are risky; they can cost you your end result, your career, your reputation, your health, your inner peace, your family, and most importantly, your ability to reach your outcome and achieve even greater heights. That is a price too high to pay.

It's OK to Start Slow

It matters not how fast you progress, only that you consistently do something towards this end. A snail moving ahead at a slow but steady pace will cross the finish line before a rabbit standing idle. When you first start, it may feel like swimming against the current. When you start a business or join the fitness club, you'll work hard but won't see any results for a while. Persist anyway.

At times, action is something akin to the growth of a bamboo plant. You can water the plant and care for it for five years, with little sign of change. However, after five years, the plant might suddenly shoot up in mere weeks. I don't want to imply that you should wait that long, especially if you don't receive any results or feedback. However, I want you to be persistent and patient because sometimes you need practice and time to build the competencies that will help you succeed.

Now, you may be wondering, *how long should this take?* I have no idea. It will take however long it takes to achieve your outcome, your big breakthrough. In a way, the journey is the reason you do what you do. It's not the result; it's the becoming who you are meant to be along the way that changes everything. Enjoy the journey.

I've been an entrepreneur for all my adult life. When I look back at my progress, I see small steps, small breakthroughs, and many mistakes. The point is to rise every day and accept that you see success when you look back and connect the dots. Had I not been on a mission, I may have given up long before I reached the outcome I so cherish. If you find yourself on a mission with nothing to show for it and want quicker results, consider spending time with a mentor or a powerful peer group that will influence and challenge you. At the very least, they will help you keep the faith and push you onward.

Results Are Just Outside of Your Comfort Zone

The bad news: when you first start, getting out of bed in the morning, pushing yourself out of your comfort zone, propelling yourself towards new successes can be hard. The good news: with daily, persistent, patient action, the pursuit of your goals will get easier and easier. Eventually, it will become a habit.

Today, it's not difficult for me to lecture. Quite the opposite. When I teach and help others, I experience a high vibration and energy; I feel positively alive. The more energy I invest, the more energy I receive. And that's absolutely fantastic. However, this wasn't always the case.

Giving my first lecture was a challenging assignment for me. But so was giving my second and my third. However, with each new step, each new lecture or workshop, things got easier. Because I had more knowledge and experience, it became simpler for me to connect with the audience. In-person workshops continue to be my preferred method of passing on knowledge and assisting people. Later, online lectures and workshops came to the fore, which was a challenge for me at first. I had to step out of my comfort zone yet again.

I had to learn the technical aspects of running an online workshop, as well as how to connect with and touch the hearts of the audience online—which was, believe me, a huge struggle at first. But since I was determined to achieve a breakthrough, I overcame my limiting beliefs around online classes. I had a vision and a plan for running them and concentrated all my efforts on how to carry out the first online workshop, and then the second, and the third, and so on.

Today, I can't imagine doing my job without sharing knowledge online, not only in my native language but also in foreign languages. I believe that the price I pay for delivering online lectures and classes is incomparably lower than the price I'd have to pay if I didn't. There are so many people, from all around the world, attending my online classes. I'd never get to meet them in person or be able to share my knowledge with them without an online platform.

Taking steps out of your comfort zone is hard. But imagine the places it might take you.

Keep Yourself Motivated Until You See Results

Action taken in a positive emotional state is one of the most important, if not *the* most important, steps towards your break-through. It's the key to your persistence, what will keep you motivated until you see results.

Every morning when you wake up, put yourself in a positive emotional state. Meditate, do some strength exercises, move your body, having allowed enough time for rest and sleep. Adjust your posture, focus your attention on what you're capable of, ask yourself good questions.

Check in with your big why (what you wrote down in Chapter 2). Are any of your old limiting beliefs cropping back up; which ones; what could you replace them with instead; are you in alignment with your value hierarchy; what might you need to adjust?

Perhaps it's time to revisit your tools: repeat powerful affirmations; engage in some self-hypnosis; replay your vision in your mind. Perhaps it would help to go back to your plan and confirm where you are along the path so you know you're taking the right steps. Consider what fresh knowledge or skill could make this easier while lighting you up. How could you make the necessary tasks fun? After all, it's much easier to act and do when you're motivated and having fun.

30- 60- 90- Day Challenges

Since consistent action requires you to move towards your objectives and aspirations every day—every day—make use of a 30, 60, or even better, a 90-day challenge, and gamify your progress.

The challenge consists of committing yourself to giving your all every day for the next 90 days (or, if you're starting small, 30 or 60 days). But you need to *do* something. Every day for the next 90 days, you must take decisive steps forward towards your breakthrough. As you start to change and consistently take purposeful action over those 90 days, things and people around you will begin to change.

Using relationships as an example, you might say: "During these 90 days, I'll pour all my love, warmth, and playfulness into my relationship; I'll be patient and understanding with my partner. Every day I'll visualize our happy, loving relationship, and accept that my partner can express their affection towards me whenever they want; most importantly, I'll maintain a positive emotional state at all times." Or, perhaps, "During the next 90 days, I'll be affectionate with my partner, finding ways to shower them with love and gratitude."

If you truly behave like this for 90 days, you'll notice a significant improvement in your love relationship. Because if you're focused on building the relationship with your partner for 90 days, you're not doing things that could endanger the relationship—you're not losing your head; you're not distracted, harsh, or judgmental. Rather, with your playfulness, love, and understanding, you'll be able to enjoy the relationship you've always dreamed of before you know it.

If you want to transform an unhealthy lifestyle, eat nutritious foods, go for a walk, go to the gym, meditate, practice yoga, get a good night's rest . . . every day, for the next 90 days.

If you want to increase sales in your company, call a certain number of clients, meet a need, improve, automate, and systemize sales, inspire your coworkers, inspire your team . . . every day, for the next 90 days.

To make the biggest possible breakthrough, what will you choose to focus on, completely, for the next 90 days?

EXERCISE: Choose your 30/60/90day challenge

1. Set the start and finish date for your challenge; write this on a piece of paper.

2. Schedule the necessary activities in your calendar.

3. What's the price you need to pay to achieve your goal?

4. What's the price you're paying now because you haven't yet achieved your goal?

5. What's the price you'll have to pay if you don't achieve your goal?

6. To whom will you dedicate this challenge?

The purpose of this challenge is for you to go above and beyond in all your daily activities in the chosen area. For instance, if you want to write a book, write five pages every single day. Don't go to bed until you've completed the five pages. In 30 days, you'll have written 150 pages. In 60 days, you'll have written 300 pages. But will this be 300 excellent pages? Certainly not. You'll have to delete, add, or replace some parts. But at least it's a very good start.

Build New Habits

Habits can help you maintain consistency in your actions and routines, which leads to increased results over time. Productive habits enable you to work smarter and accomplish more, to make better use of resources.

When you develop and maintain those habits, it offers numerous benefits. You'll be better equipped to streamline actions, which allows you to perform tasks automatically and with minimal effort. This increased efficiency will save you time and mental energy, enabling you to focus on what matters most.

Habits can serve as coping mechanisms for managing stress and anxiety, help you build self-discipline, and strengthen your ability to resist temptations that will lead you nowhere. They provide structure and momentum, especially when they're aligned with your goals and priorities.

Developing new habits requires consistency, motivation, and a structured approach. Here are some strategies to help you easily develop new habits:

1. Begin by focusing on one small habit.

Don't try to change everything at once. Having a manageable task increases your chances of success and helps build momentum over time.

2. Clearly define the habit you want to develop.

When you do this, you can set positive, measurable, time-bound, and personally relevant goals. Having a clear vision of what you want to achieve will keep you motivated and focused.

3. Incorporate the new habit into your daily or weekly routine.

This is how to make it easier to remember and stick to it. Choose a specific time, location, or trigger to cue the behavior and make it a consistent part of your day.

4. Formulate "if-then" statements that link the new habit to a specific cue or situation.

For example, "If it's 7 a.m., then I will go for a twenty-minute walk." This helps automate the behavior and makes it easier to follow through.

5. Find "anchor" points to link new habits.

You can do this by identifying existing habits or routines that you already have in place and pairing the new habit with it. This pairing can help reinforce the behavior and make it more automatic.

6. Create a pairing rule.

Connect a new habit with an existing one where you can only do the old habit after you complete the new one. For example, you can only brush your teeth (old habit) after you meditated for ten minutes (new habit).

7. Keep track of your habit development journey by using a habit tracker or journal.

Seeing your progress visually can provide motivation and accountability; it also allows you to identify patterns and areas for improvement.

8. Be consistent.

This is key. Make a commitment to practice the habit every day or on a regular schedule, even if it's just for a few minutes. Over time, consistent repetition will help solidify the habit.

9. Reinforce the habit by rewarding yourself for sticking to it.

Celebrate your successes, no matter how small, and acknowledge the progress you've made. Rewards can be simple, such as a pat on the back, a treat, or a break.

10. Be flexible and willing to adapt your approach as needed.

If you encounter obstacles or setbacks, don't be discouraged. Instead, learn from them, adjust your strategy if necessary, and keep moving forward.

11. Share your goals.

Allow your friends, family, or a support group to encourage and hold you accountable. Having a support system can provide motivation, guidance, and accountability on your habit development journey.

12. Be patient.

Remember what they say, it takes ninety or more days to get used to a new identity, which is the most powerful shift when it comes to changing habits.

By incorporating these strategies into your daily life, you can make it easier to develop new habits and create positive changes that stick over the long term. Remember to be patient with yourself and celebrate your progress along the way.

Overshoot the Mark

It may be OK to take small steps toward your goal (with the understanding that those steps must be consistent), but I'm also a huge fan of overshooting the mark, of doing far more than is expected of you so that you achieve your big breakthrough faster.

Have a bigger vision, a bigger goal. If you want a million dollars, aim for five million because reaching higher will create a different thinking process, a different energy to fuel your actions. You're going to consistently do what you need to do with that bigger goal in place. Dreaming bigger and aiming higher is a source of rocket fuel.

Now, going the extra mile is a component of overshooting the mark. Going the extra mile means doing more, giving more of yourself than is required. If your basketball coach says you must do 100 foul shots, you shoot 110. If your boss expects you to make 100 phone calls, you make 150. If they suggest reading 100 books to become an expert in your field, read 200.

You'll discover the extra mile route is never crowded. Most people don't want to dispense the added effort. They only want to do what is absolutely necessary, if that. That's why those who go above and beyond are far more successful.

Consider this: What difference would it make if you added something extra to what you already offer your clients? A written note, a Christmas card, a call—just to touch base, a tiny symbol of your gratitude.

An additional action can be small—it doesn't have to expend a lot of extra time, money, or energy, but can make a dramatic impact. And overshooting your mark, well, that can lead to an extravagant kind of success.

EXERCISE: Go the Extra Mile

1. Write down in what way you can go the extra mile in the area where you want to make a breakthrough.

Put yourself in a good emotional state and step towards your desired results and dreams. Imperfect action today is far better than perfect action tomorrow (or never). Start today, start now. Concentrate on the step you must take right now. You have the resources, capabilities, knowledge, and everything else you need. I'll say it again: trust you'll learn the necessary steps that follow along the way. Let's go, action!

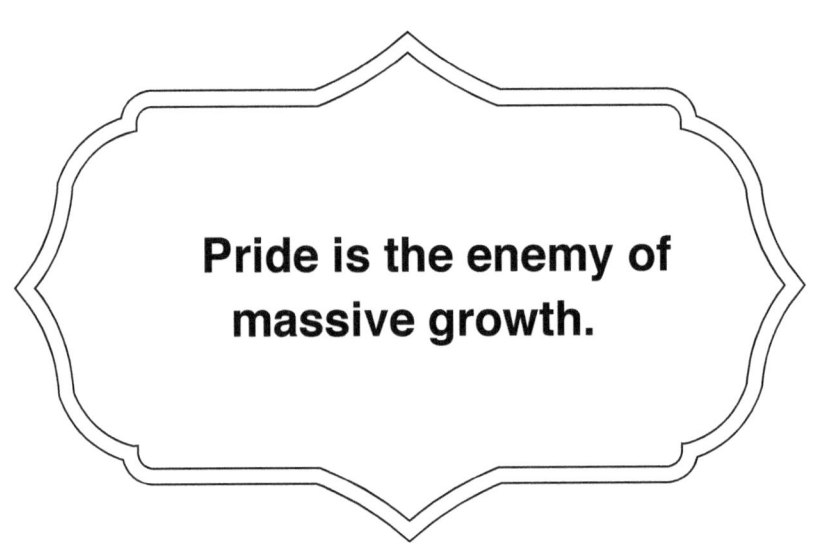

Pride is the enemy of
massive growth.

9

KEEP LEARNING

———

Education is the most powerful weapon you can use to change the world.
–Nelson Mandela

With an elevation of 9,395 feet, Triglav is the highest mountain in Slovenia and the highest peak of the Julian Alps. The mountain is the pre-eminent symbol of the Slovene nation, appearing on the coat of arms and flag of Slovenia. It is the centerpiece of Triglav National Park, one of the oldest national parks in Europe. About 80,000 people from all around the world climb Mount Triglav each year.

Now, there are plenty of marked routes leading to the summit of Triglav. Unfortunately, the most popular routes (which are not very technically demanding) include steep and exposed sections that should never be underestimated. This means you want to know where you are going and what you are doing if you're looking to avoid unnecessary unpleasantness or a full-blown emergency.

Before taking on the challenge, it would certainly pay to do some research online. While making your way to the top, carry a map (assuming you know how to read a map, of course). Without a baseline expertise in planning such an endeavor, hiring a good guide would make a lot of sense, too. Learning about the trails from someone who has been there before will not only save you a significant amount of time and energy but also improve the likelihood of reaching the summit quickly and safely.

Let's see where we are on the current roadmap, the one that leads to your massive success. You've made a decision, firmed up your internal model of the world—aligning your values and beliefs to your vision, freed yourself from limiting beliefs, got to know your vision—what it looks, tastes, feels, and smells like—created some sort of plan, abandoned distractions to focus on the tasks at hand, agreed to pay the price and do what's required. Which leads us here, to gaining knowledge so you are equipped to continue traveling up this unfamiliar path.

You may be tempted to think that you have it all together, that you don't need to learn anymore. But if you're going to make it to the summit, you're going to need additional resources to further catalyze your growth.

When you constantly learn, constantly improve, and constantly change, you will gain the competitive advantage you're seeking. And there are lots of ways to learn: reading books, taking courses, listening to podcasts, studying and modeling experts, attending seminars, hiring a pro, and so on. Yes, this requires an investment of your time, energy, and perhaps your money, but can you think of a better use of your resources?

Today, I'm more driven than ever to keep learning. Not a day goes by when I don't learn something new. Even when I'm on vacation, I'm expanding my knowledge. Sometimes I read or write something, and other times I listen to a recording. I get my information in a variety of ways, both online and in person. I'm constantly surrounded by a variety of coaches and mentors. I learn from them, and they assist me in pursuing my vision and achieving results. They also teach me how to take the knowledge and information I've obtained from a variety of sources, from all over the world, and pass it along to my workshop participants.

Yet it is incredibly easy to think that you need no further inspiration, training, skill-sharpening—whatever you want to call it—when you are on the long and winding path. Heed my warning.

A while ago, I ran across a participant from one of the first workshops I ever attended. She'd been just as enthusiastic as me all those years ago. However, the woman who stood before me now was in a rather poor emotional state. She stated that she had learned everything she ever needed to know during that workshop. We talked for a while, and she admitted that she had challenges with her health, career, and relationships. Yet it made no sense to her to devote further time, money, or energy to improving or educating herself. I couldn't help thinking that the price she was paying was considerably higher than the price she would have paid to attend the same seminars and workshops to which I had availed myself. Not taking action was far more expensive for her than actually doing something to build on her baseline knowledge.

The truth of the matter is, there is always more to learn. Personally, I've never had more knowledge than I do now, yet I'm also aware that there is so much more I know nothing about. It astounds me every day how many things I didn't know! Chances are good, the same can be said of you. But with continued learning, you might just uncover one of those black holes.

Learn From Others

Hiring a guide, the way you would for a mountain expedition doesn't make you a loser; it allows you to fill a gap in your knowledge and experience and come away with a sense of accomplishment and far more confidence. Yes, there's much learning you can do on your own, and I'll get to that shortly. But I want to first emphasize the true benefits you can gain from bringing in outside help.

A good mentor or coach has been where you are now. They've seen, faced, and overcome the very same obstacles. They can help you avoid them by pointing out useful detours (if you will). They may be able to see things like your limiting beliefs better than you if only because they're second nature to you and you're not even aware of them. Which is another aspect of learning from others: humility. You've got to put your pride aside and listen to (learn from) constructive feedback.

Yet people are often too proud to dig deeper into things they don't fully understand or to seek outside help. They want to present an outer appearance of power and invulnerability even when they're attempting things they've never done before. Pride is the enemy of massive growth. Pride costs you big.

Sometimes, all you need to do is ask for help. Ask for help from someone who has already overcome the kind of challenge you're now facing. Ask for help from someone who is more successful than you and learn how to tackle the problem or challenge at hand. All your problems have already been solved. Sometimes all you need is one piece of advice, one word, or one opportunity.

Surround Yourself With Smart People

Speaking of getting outside help . . . it was motivational speaker Jim Rohn who once said that we're the average of the five people we spend the most time with. We learn from them whether we realize it or not. That's why you want to surround yourself with people who support your goals and reinforce positive beliefs. The goal is to minimize exposure to negative influences, seek out sources of inspiration, encouragement, and support, and learn things you wouldn't learn on your own.

We often tell our children that who they hang out with is important because they'll adopt thought patterns and behaviors of those around them without even realizing it. The same holds true for you. So, surround yourself with skilled, driven, and action oriented individuals.

You may be tempted to surround yourself with people who are similar to you. We are prone to "recruit" individuals who think like us because we can predict (and therefore manage) them more easily. But in doing so, you won't learn much or advance as an individual. You want to find people who will stretch you and help you grow. For example, if you're a dreamer, you may need to be around a realist, and vice versa.

Nowadays, technology allows you to surround yourself with individuals to whom you wouldn't otherwise have access. The mastermind concept, attributed to Napoleon Hill, is one of the most effective ways to solve the dilemmas and challenges you may face. Hill explains in his book, *Think and Grow Rich*, that Henry Ford, Harvey Firestone, and Thomas Edison created their own mastermind group. The concept was very simple. The group met once a week to discuss their goals and the challenges they were encountering in their businesses. They assisted each other by offering suggestions to help each other's businesses flourish. At their regular meetings, when they discussed their business concepts and explored new market ideas, they recognized a strategic advantage and an opportunity for quicker expansion.

The mastermind concept involves regular meetings of three to five people. The members can meet on a weekly to monthly basis, or a few times a year, and the meetings can be held online or in person. At each meeting, a current challenge is posed by one member of the group; the other members respond without judgement, outlining how they'd tackle the challenge or solve the problem. If the group has six members, you now have five potential solutions to your problem or five responses to your question. But, of course, it's up to you whether to apply those ideas and solve your challenge in practice.

Maybe you already know who you'd want to meet on a regular basis to discuss your objectives, vision, and strategy, or to solicit feedback on current difficulties in your life. Call that person, explain the mastermind concept, and ask them if they want to take part in your group. Agree that both of you will invite one more person to the group, and you'll have four members.

Invite people who are successful in their fields. It's not necessary that all members are from the same industry or background. In fact, I advise the contrary. This is because when members operate in a variety of ways, they bring new knowledge and concepts to your model of the world and help you look at your problem from entirely different viewpoints.

Ever since I started my entrepreneurial journey, I've been a member of more than one mastermind group at the same time. I'm constantly in contact with people who are more successful than I am. And from the invaluable knowledge and great encouragement gained, I recommend you do the same. The purpose of your breakthrough (or breakthroughs) isn't only to attain a certain result, but to become the person you want to be. And mastermind groups can be quite useful in that regard.

Turn Learning Into a Project

There are some things others can help you with, and there are some things you must take on alone. You must make learning a personal project for yourself. You must have a specific objective in mind.

When it comes to learning, your intelligence quotient (IQ) and the ability to learn quickly aren't that important. Because it's common for people with a strong desire to learn to outperform brilliant and capable people who have long since ceased studying on a continuous and persistent basis. Even if you study every day—and I mean every day—for the rest of your life, there will be many valuable and intriguing topics yet to discover. It's critical that you study continuously and persistently in the subject matter you genuinely want to master.

Your Learning Plan

What would you need to learn in order to quit your dead-end job and start your own company? Hard skills might include learning how to develop a comprehensive business plan that outlines your company's mission, vision, goals, target market, competitive analysis, marketing strategy, operations plan, financial projections, and growth strategy. You would certainly want to learn how to conduct market research to identify potential customers, understand their needs and preferences, assess market trends, and evaluate the competitive landscape. You might want to gain knowledge and skills in product or service development, including idea generation, prototyping, testing, refinement, and scaling. Legal and regulatory compliance, basic accounting principles, financial management techniques . . . the list goes on and on.

This means you must educate yourself. Read books. Listen to audio recordings and podcasts. Take part in workshops or courses. Connect and hang out with people who share your interests, as well as those who have already accomplished what you aspire to. Get yourself a coach. Get yourself several coaches. Get yourself a mentor. Invest in yourself. Schedule time in your calendar to learn and improve. All worthwhile activities if you want to make a breakthrough.

And I know what you're thinking: I don't have the time. This is a lie because we all have time for what truly matters.

I invite you to commit at least fifteen minutes (or even twenty or thirty minutes) each day to your education. You can do that, can't you?

Take an online course and break it into manageable chunks. Plan for when you want to listen to, learn, and absorb new knowledge throughout the day. This could be in the morning, during the day, during a brief break in the afternoon, or in the evening before going to bed. Find the time that suits you best. If you're not sure what time will work best for you, try out several. Listen to educational content for thirty days in the morning, thirty days while commuting to and from work, thirty days when resting or walking, and thirty days before going to bed. Take note of the time window that is most effective for you. Drop what doesn't work and stick with what does.

Today, it's easier than ever to combine learning with other activities: while you brush your teeth you can listen to a podcast; while you work out you can listen to a motivational speech. Such inspiration will open your bandwidth for learning the hard skills. You can start a morning ritual in which you work out—do yoga, walk on the treadmill—while you watch an educational video or speak your goals, dreams, plans, or vision out loud.

Sometimes I learn in a completely different way: I listen to stillness. In this way, you program your day. You can listen to educational information while driving, walking, or taking public transportation to and from work. Transform your car into a university on four wheels, and as you drive listen to material that will help you reach your goals faster.

As a result, over the next five years, you'll become exceptionally adept, if not remarkable, in the area you're relentlessly educating yourself about every single day. In ten years, you'll have accumulated sufficient extra miles of learning and improvement to consider yourself one of the world's top experts in your field. This is a small price to pay for the wealth of knowledge you'll acquire.

EXERCISE: Plan Your Learning

1. What else do you want or need to learn?

2. Who can you ask for help?

3. Schedule time in your calendar to devote to further learning.

When You Don't Know What You Don't Know

Oftentimes, people don't realize what might be valuable and transformative for them. If they did know, they'd seek out this knowledge, study it, and apply it to their life. The worst thing that can happen to you is that you're aware that you don't know something and still do nothing about it; hence, you're your own greatest obstacle to advancement.

To get at that trove of things you do not yet know, adopt an outsider's perspective. Look at your business, your relationships, and yourself from afar, as an observer. Take time to reflect. *If someone else was looking at my life, my way of doing things, what might they suggest I do differently?*

Of course, another way to get at what you don't yet know is to make mistakes along the way.

Charles Darwin stated that it's not the strongest species that survives, nor the most intelligent or the fastest. The species that survive are those that are most adaptable to change.

When it comes to change, mistakes are part of the package. Experts learn from their mistakes, and so should you. Look at your slipups as opportunities to achieve greater levels of success and recognize the insights gained through unexpected falls. You'll come to regard them as blessings. It won't be the end of the world if you stumble now and then. What matters is that you get back up every time you fall and let the fall help you improve. Falling usually indicates you need to learn something new.

If you haven't noticed before, failure can be uncomfortable to us mere mortals. But success requires you to embrace it—especially when you step out of your comfort zone, do something you've never done before, push your boundaries, seek out opportunities for growth, and move in their direction. This is how you become the best version of yourself.

Every mistake you've made in the past can add to your know-how. Don't make the same mistakes twice but be grateful for the learning. Don't make it hard to admit your mistakes. There's nothing wrong with lapses in reasoning, or trying something that doesn't work, as long as you tried your best. Learn what works best for you and move on.

There will also come a time when you find yourself in a situation where you can't see a way out, or you can't endure any longer. Don't panic. There's a solution to every problem. Most of the time, you can't fix the problem at the level it was created, which is where true learning comes in. Instead of beating yourself up, discover a new way—change your state and how you look at the situation, so you can find your way to a solution with far more ease. So, allow me to beat this drum again. Be a lifelong learner: take part in training and education; hire the coach or mentor; take action; keep up to date. If you don't, it could take five or ten years (maybe even more) to move ahead in life; worse yet, it may keep you from ever reaching your breakthrough. It may seem a higher price to pay, but in the end—for all the benefits it affords you—you're sure to find it a bargain.

Pay it forward.

10

CREATE A MISSION TO GIVE BACK

_____

A leader is one who knows the way, goes the way,
and shows the way.
–John C. Maxwell

Making a breakthrough is frequently difficult at first; it involves a great deal of emotional and physical effort, as well as commitment, hard work, discipline, and focus. When you achieve this breakthrough, however, you experience enormous rewards. Don't keep it to yourself. Share the benefits with others. When you serve and help others, when you give back—when you start or cocreate a movement of goodness—you discover even more meaning and strength to find your own way.

If you're at the beginning, and your next step involves liberating yourself from limiting beliefs, the idea of creating a movement may seem a bit daunting, even farfetched. But hear me out. Helping others will give you incredible energy and unexpected opportunities.

And just because you make it your mission to help others, doesn't mean you have it all together. Even after you've made your first breakthrough, there will be challenges. That's life. But if you can find a way to maintain your focus on your vision, while giving your time and resources to others, challenges will become simpler to overcome, and you'll grow in ways you never dreamed possible.

Make It Your Mission

Everybody has the potential to help others. Not only that, if you have the knowledge, power, talent, and skills to improve your own life, you have an obligation to help others.

And there's no lack of opportunities. Wherever you look, around every corner, there's a way for you to improve the world and make it a better place. Consider the difficulties that people face throughout the world: some are lonely, obese, or sick; some suffer ridicule, abuse, or mistreatment; some lack the opportunity for an education; some face financial difficulties. The list goes on and on.

Consider how you might be able to assist along the way, without expectation of anything in return. Then, commit to it.

Just like you commit to your vision, commit to making the lives of those around you better than they were before. Commit to doing good. Commit to becoming the best version of yourself—and commit to helping others be the same.

Trust me when I say, this commitment will help keep you going, even when things get tough.

My Mission in Action

Sometimes it makes me sad when I see all the needs of the world, and how few possibilities I have to meet them. In the past, this used to be a source of great frustration. But then I heard the words of songwriter and educator, Jana Stanfield, "You can't do all the good that the world needs, but the world needs all the good that you can do."

It was then I realized I couldn't assist everyone, but if I helped one person, one child, this world would be a better place. So, I considered my experience, my interests—where I might be able to lend a hand . . .

I want to provide children with the opportunity to develop life skills that will help them overcome the obstacles and challenges that life will throw at them. It's vital to teach children how to do something, rather than simply meeting an immediate need. There's no doubt that we must provide the basic necessities of life for all children, such as food, shelter, clothing, and so on. But at the same time, we must give them the knowledge and resources required to survive even when we're not around.

Since hypnosis and unconscious programming techniques helped me develop my own skills and deal with challenges, I'm continuously thinking of how to pass this information on to youngsters. My company provides seminars for children and teenagers who want to shift their beliefs; we offer participants in our seminars and workshops the opportunity to send their children to our kids' program for free or in return for a donation to a selected charity.

Even writing this book is a way for me to help others. By sharing what I've learned, I'm not only helping you, but the people with whom you share your life.

In addition, my company participates in philanthropic projects; we've provided gifts to special needs children in various schools and supported the construction of schools in Kenya; we find ways to support the local community and assist families with social and financial difficulties.

I'm not saying this to brag. God, the Universe, this planet, and the community in which I live have provided me with all the support I require. I'm simply returning the favor. I'm sharing this to illustrate how giving back can become a part of the very fabric of your vision and breakthrough.

What Can You Do?

There are many ways to help, where do you even begin?

You can start with a simple smile. Smile at the person you see in the mirror each morning; at a stranger on the street; at the person serving at the bakery; at the youngster who is observing you with interest. If that person returns your smile, you'll smile even more. Not only that, both you and the person to whom you gifted the smile will feel much better. What you give to others you give to yourself because we're all connected. Think you might feel a little less lonely and unsure in the process?

You can start with your family. Ensure your spouse has the love and resources to see their own dreams come to fruition; devote your energy to raising positive, honest, and happy children. If you've set out to create deep bonds with those you love, imagine how such focus could yield immeasurable returns.

You can start with your local community. Grow healthy, organic fruits and vegetables and share them with your neighbors; join a volunteer crew to clean up area parks; participate in social activities, such as singing in a local choir. If your goal is to get fit and/or to develop fulfilling relationships, these activities could support that end, and more . . .

Over time you can expand the ways you give back. You can contribute time, money, and experience; you can write and publish a book; you can host seminars and workshops.

The format isn't important. Look for needs that speak most to you—and find your own format for doing good. Test out various things to see which brings you the greatest satisfaction, joy, and good energy.

In short, do as Maya Angelou suggested, "Try to be a rainbow in somebody else's cloud." Be on constant lookout for ways to help. Make the world a better place. And you just might find that the more lives you support, the more life will support you.

Pay It Forward

You're probably familiar with the concept of "paying it forward." It's when someone receives an act of kindness and does something kind for another person, instead of merely receiving or repaying the original good deed.

The source of this concept was a fictional twelve-year-old boy who lived alone with his mother. He was given a school assignment to come up with an idea for changing the world for the better. He was also asked to put his idea into practice. The boy came up with something simple yet very effective. He began to do good deeds for people chosen at random. He named his plan *Pay it Forward*, which is also the title of the movie based on the novel of the same name. The boy's school project turned into a movement that began to change the world for the better.

Paying it forward is a good way for you to change the world for the better, as well.

As you've seen, success is not accomplished alone. Countless people will assist you in your breakthroughs throughout your lifetime—they'll support and encourage, offer constructive criticism and help redirect, provide resources, and give you tools to grow (in person and online; directly and through books, podcasts, and workshops).

Pass on that knowledge and support.

Start a Movement

The funny thing about being committed to making a difference in your home, community, nation, world, is that it can be catching. Get one person enthused about your idea and it leaves the door open for others to follow. Before long, countless others are joining in your cause; they're joining in your pursuit to do good. And a movement is born.

You don't want to give to charity or participate in social or environmental projects purely to gain followers. It shouldn't be done for marketing purposes, to boost your ego, or with the expectation of public acclaim. You do it because it's the right thing to do. But it's a good idea to understand how a movement works—how one person can inspire others to join a cause, and the work snowballs.

So, while nobody needs to know all the ways you give back, you shouldn't be afraid to share it. There may be those who are not sure who or how to help; your example may be what gets them started. They may be waiting for your invitation. The movement you start together may be the very thing to spark great, lasting change.

Even if that movement does not reach its pinnacle or fully blossom in your lifetime, you can know your actions have kindled a ray of hope for our planet. Share what you have learned. Teach another to do what you have done. The world needs you. It needs your energy; it needs your positivity. The world needs your movement. There are countless others who could use your assistance in one way or another: nature, animals, the elderly, children, people living in poverty. It doesn't matter how much you contribute; what matters is that you pay attention to those in need.

EXERCISE: Your Mission to Pay It Forward

What does it mean to you to help others?

1. In what ways could you contribute to doing good?

2. Who do you want to help? How could you start a movement to make the world a better place?

Courage isn't the absence of fear but the ability to move forward despite it.

CONCLUSION

Everything you have ever wanted is on the other side of fear.
–**George Adair**

Years ago, a young, handicapped man who couldn't use his arms and also walked with difficulty, attended one of my workshops. He wanted to pursue his dream of becoming a singer, but he was terrified of being on stage in front of an audience, which is something you must get comfortable with if you're going to perform. While he was working on his fear, he met another attendee, a blind girl, who had come to overcome her own resistance to public speaking. The two ended up joining forces and began singing together, getting booked on different stages far and wide. They subsequently became a couple and had a baby daughter. They will often come back and tell their story to motivate others. He will say that she has become his hands, and she claims he became her eyes. They complement each other beautifully, providing strengths the other can lean on. Instead of being victims because of their physical limitations, they decided to be victors.

Sometimes people come to a workshop for one reason, only to discover the real reason they came—something so far removed from what they imagined, but a thousand times better than what they could have hoped. Maybe they're looking for a way to change their values, overcome a limiting belief, lock onto a vision that will pull them forward; but God, or the Universe, or whatever higher intelligence is out there, shifts them in a far better way.

What is possible for you is even bigger and grander than you currently think, too.

But trusting in a guiding force does not excuse you from doing the work: making a decision, setting your sights, making a plan, taking action . . .

Stay Disciplined

Why would you expect to have discipline if you don't know what you want in life; why would you expect to have discipline if you don't know what it will be like when you get to your final destination? Think about it. What on earth could motivate you enough to do anything that might make you uncomfortable? It makes no sense. Yet without discipline, everything you set out to do will somehow peter out before you get any kind of momentum going. You'll look for every possible excuse to justify your lack of action and your dreary status quo.

You need your thoughts, decisions, and actions to point in the direction you want, to achieve your breakthrough.

Sometimes all it takes to get started is to wake up and realize that you are your biggest enemy. You are the one who creates the barriers in your path with your thoughts and limitations. You need to realize a new life is possible, that a breakthrough is well within your reach. And you need to do so before an illness, painful ordeal, job loss, or other discomfort forces your hand. You will need discipline to wrench you out of your comfort zone.

Embrace Your New Story

I've shown you how to remove the obstacles and limiting beliefs that keep you small, to access your unconscious mind to automate the process of achievement—how to get rid of the old memories, thoughts, and beliefs that are holding you back and create a brand new and much more powerful story of who you are and what you're capable of.

This new story will give you courage, despite your fears (most of which stem from your limiting beliefs or misaligned values, anchors and strategies, and your current identity). This new story will guide you through your current obstacles, negative feedback, and the lack of information, skills, or helpful role models. This new story will silence the inner voice that's holding you back from making a breakthrough and moving toward your goals and desired results. This new story will transform your identity, redefine who you are in the field where you want to make a breakthrough.

Continually Clarify Your Vision

You now know the component pieces to a solid vision, too—how to replay vivid images over and over in your head to catalyze action. This vision should include becoming someone who's healthy, vital, and always learning, someone who will diligently undertake the mundane activities that will lead to the desired outcome, every day. It's more than having the end goal in mind; you must envision the everyday tasks, the small breakthroughs that will lead to the big breakthrough you want to achieve. Believe in your vision, believe in your grand dreams. Fill your thoughts with the belief that you're capable of making your dreams a reality. Remember, the more action you take, the more you will learn and the clearer your vision will be.

If you aren't crystal clear yet about your vision, if you don't quite know where you want to go, make it your primary goal to create clarity in your life. Take a step back and make the decision that you'll do everything you can to create this compelling ideal.

Follow Your Plan

Stay committed to your vision and what you want to achieve; continually improve; and execute the plan. Akin to a GPS, your plan will remind you of your destination. You will need the reminder.

When you put your plan into action, you will find yourself being guided to take the most effective and efficient actions to reach your goals quicker, with less resistance. You'll be astonished at what you can accomplish if you persist with it.

Remember, it's sufficient to have a clear plan for your next steps. You'll find acting and taking the plunge, even when not totally prepared, will give you more breakthroughs and opportunities to learn than staying put in the thinking, planning, and mulling over phase. You can continue to update the plan, enhance it, and move forward.

Act, Learn, Share

The key to getting results is taking action. Because when you act and go the extra mile with a smile on your face and in a good emotional state, your chances of achieving the desired goal are greatly increased. You now know that by changing your behavior you can achieve your intended results and goals.

Take advantage of every free moment to gain new knowledge and thereby enrich your life and the lives of the people you care about. Connect the big results you want in your life to your life's purpose.

Finally, cultivate a practice of gratitude. Be more present in your life; direct more intentional thought and action towards the people you care about most; honor the good you already have in your life.

Forget about Overnight Success

When you decide to pursue a breakthrough, and I know you will, don't expect to achieve success overnight. Life isn't a straight line; it's a winding path through hills and valleys, with ups and downs. There will be challenges. There will be problems. Solving them is what will make you grow.

In a podcast interview I listened to recently, psychiatrist Phil Stutz spoke of three important truths about life: pain, uncertainty, the need for constant work. In a nutshell, it's fine to have goals and ambitions, but if you are under the illusion that money, success, power, or status will absolve you of these three truths, not only will you be disappointed, but you'll also likely suffer resentment and anger, which impairs your happiness.

Instead of fostering such illusions, tie or wedge your goals and ambitions to meaning, purpose, and service. Find ways to gird your life to something that's personally meaningful, to find a way to give back in service to others. Rise above ego, cultivate a personal faith. Understand that there's more to this short life than your individual concerns.

Also, keep in mind that every day a new breakthrough might occur. Successes do not always feel like breakthroughs. They may feel more like failures, as though you accomplished nothing or that you squandered your day, with no discernible results. Follow the plan; take action. Trust it.

And when you begin to doubt yourself, look back to where you were at the same time one year ago. As Steve Jobs said in his famous Stanford commencement speech, "You can't connect the dots looking forward; you can only connect them looking backwards."

Even if you're taking the smallest consistent steps, you'll be moving forward.

Do Not Compare Yourself to Others

At times, you may be tempted to look at the stride others are taking and feel inferior. Don't give in to temptation. Every move, every breakthrough is unique—even your own.

You are the only person you should compare yourself to, how you were yesterday versus how you are today. Everyone has a story and each story is different. You may be able to jump right out of bed, unaware of the breakthrough you have achieved; another person may suffer from a debilitating disease that makes getting out of bed the largest breakthrough they can imagine. It makes no sense to compare the two.

On the flip side, your breakthroughs may not make sense to others; they may think them pointless. It doesn't matter. You do not have to prove yourself to anyone. Each step you take, each achievement, is your breakthrough. It need only make sense to *you*.

Lastly, don't compare your own breakthroughs, one to another. Breakthroughs come in all sizes—immense and small, and everything in between. They serve unique purposes, too. Your first breakthrough may pale in comparison to the breakthroughs you make years from now, at the height of your success. Yet it's just as valuable, if not more so. Focus on what's in front of you.

Be Grateful

Every evening, think of all your breakthroughs for that day. And be grateful. Be grateful: for each small step you take, for life, for getting out of bed in the morning, for food and clean drinking water, for everything you have, even if you don't have as much as you'd like. Be grateful for your capabilities, for the opportunities that came your way.

To remind yourself, track your daily accomplishments. Write down at least three things, events, people for which you're grateful. Even if they appear insignificant, write them down. One day, you'll look back to discover even the smallest, most ordinary breakthroughs were important points on the road to your success. You'll also see how gratitude magnetized success.

Use Your Gifts

You were given many gifts when you were born—most of which have not fully been used. To make the most of your opportunities, use what you've already been given.

If you have a knack for speaking, speak; if you're gifted in writing, write. Maybe you're unsure about your gifts. They might not be so obvious. Reach out and ask others what they think they are. Try new things and consider what comes naturally and what you enjoy doing. Your gifts might reveal themselves while you're in action.

And don't forget to share your gifts with others. The more people you assist in the breakthroughs of others, the faster you'll accomplish your own. Share your message, energy, and potential with the rest of the world. Every time you share your knowledge with someone else—like I'm doing now—you're solidifying and clarifying it. When you share your expertise, you open the door to fresh knowledge, possibilities, and breakthroughs, as well as to becoming a better version of yourself. When you assist others in ascending to a higher level, you open the way for yourself to advance higher. You can't progress or achieve a breakthrough if you only think about yourself.

Act, Don't Just Study

The aim of knowledge is not to simply be able to regurgitate what you've heard (as teachers frequently assume) but to modify your behavior based on the information you've gained. Its purpose is to assist you in changing your behavior and therefore achieving your intended goals.

If you know something but don't do it, it means you need to repeat what you learned on the subject. Go over it again, every word and sentence, until it reaches your cells and your unconscious—until you achieve the desired change in behavior.

That means reading this book is not enough, attending a workshop is not the answer—unless it propels you to do something, to make a change for the better. You must implement what you've learned, or it is all but useless.

Take the First Step Now

There is no perfect time to choose your big breakthrough. Now is always the right time. You simply need to trust—in life and in yourself—and take the first step. It's critical to begin, despite your fears. Begin and you'll be able to progress, step by step.

Don't let uncertainty be an excuse for inaction. You were given your challenges, difficulties, or trials because you're capable of mastering them. Believe that it's possible and that you have within you the strength and ability to do it. Because you do. You are the master of your life. Nobody else has the strength to do it in your place.

It's no coincidence this book is in your hands right now.

Listen to the calling inside you. Say these words aloud:

If not now, when?

I've waited long enough!

I've been putting this off for too long.

I've made enough excuses.

Yes, I'm doing this. I'll reach a break-through!

I'll get my breakthrough. Let's go!

You have within you all it takes to accomplish a breakthrough. Start using your potential—don't wait a second longer. You're one choice away from a new beginning, one commitment away from a new life. Turn your limitations into advantages. Stop blaming, stop being a victim. Take full responsibility for your life and become a victor. Your time is limited, make the best of it. Choose your happiness; choose your joy. Choose you. Make that choice and stick to that commitment. It all starts with you and the pursuit of your breakthrough.

I sincerely, from the bottom of my heart,
wish you many little, big, and great breakthroughs.
Be happy, enjoy life, and decide to create a breakthrough *now*!
I know you can do it.

APPENDIX: THE SHIFT MODEL

———

While the strategies in the main chapters provide a wide-ranging framework for transformation, the S.H.I.F.T. model I developed zooms in on the emotional and cognitive states that often hold us back, offering a practical and structured pathway to navigate these challenges. Think of this appendix as a bonus tool—a hands-on companion to the core teachings of this book. It's particularly valuable for readers who want a clear, actionable guide to reclaim control over their thoughts and emotions while implementing the book's broader principles.

Moving from a victim mindset to a victor mindset is a journey that requires deliberate steps. To help you navigate this, here are the five *S.H.I.F.T.* stages of transformation:

S - **Suffering:** Feeling stuck in sadness, fear, or guilt.

H - **Hostility:** Blaming others and feeling anger or frustration.

I - **Insight:** Recognizing that victimhood isn't serving you.

F - **Focus:** Asking better questions and seeking solutions.

T - **Transformation:** Finding deeper meaning and embracing life's purpose.

By progressing through these stages, you can reclaim control over your thoughts and emotions, transforming your perspective from "life is happening to me" to "life is happening for me."

To better understand these stages, let's take a closer look.

Suffering stage

In this stage, people play the role of a victim. They are feeling sad, afraid, guilty. They ask questions such as: *why is this happening to me; what if people will laugh at me; what have I done wrong?* The emotion is negative, people are stuck and instead of doing something creative or productive, they do nothing. Mostly they are unaware that they are stuck in the role of a victim.

Hostility stage

In this stage, people feel that somebody else is responsible for their current situation and they are angry about it. They ask questions such as: *how can they do that to me; why are they so mean?* Being angry is a better emotion than being sad, but still, it does not serve you. When people in this stage are confronted about playing the role of victim, they will be in denial and even angrier.

Insight stage

In this stage, people finally realize that whatever they are experiencing or feeling is their doing. They become aware that this kind of thinking is not only harmful to them but is leading them away from their goals and dreams. They ask questions such as: *is this worth it; is there a better way of looking at this situation?* They are looking for a different approach.

Focus stage

In this stage, people begin asking better questions. They ask questions such as: *what can I do with the resources I have; how can I focus on something positive, creative?* Rather than focusing on the limitations and feeling a victim, they focus on what they can do. They take responsibility for their emotions and their results. This change in focus leads to positive activity that can bring the desired result.

Transformation stage

In this stage, people are all about finding a deeper and higher meaning. They shift their focus from "life is happening to me" to "life is happening for me." They are looking for a purpose beyond themselves. They serve others. They not only look to change their own lives for the better but to help others do the same.

To learn more about the S.H.I.F.T. model, go to
https://www.aleksandersinigoj.com/victor

ABOUT THE AUTHOR

DR. ALEKSANDER ŠINIGOJ is a speaker and expert in personal and business growth. He assists both local and international business executives, physicians, athletes, psychologists, entrepreneurs, and others in achieving better results. He has worked for renowned companies in Slovenia and overseas and lectured on four continents and in many countries around the world. The author of several audio and video programs, books, and innovative approaches, he helps individuals achieve their goals through positive transformation.

Aleksander Šinigoj is a man of practice; he puts what he teaches into action in his own life. He believes in the enormous potential of each person, and the chance for growth and development. Experience firsthand how he can assist you and your coworkers in achieving better results and a different way of thinking. Invite him to your company or join one of his workshops, in person or online.

BONUS

It's time to rewrite your story. Become the victor of your own journey and step boldly into the future you deserve. Finally, enjoy the results you most desire. It's time to access the free resources I mentioned throughout the book to further assist you as you do the work of leveling up and owning the outcome you most desire. Go to https://www.aleksandersinigoj.com/victor

www.ingramcontent.com/pod-product-compliance
Lightning Source LLC
Chambersburg PA
CBHW060419130626
46555CB00005B/2132